Ordering
Your Private World

Ordering
Your Private World
ANNIVERSARY EDITION

by
Gordon MacDonald

This Special Cell Leader's Edition Is Available From:
TOUCH Publications
P.O. Box 19888 • Houston, TX 77224
Tel: 713-497-7901 • Fax: 713-497-0904

OLIVER
NELSON

THOMAS NELSON PUBLISHERS
Nashville • Atlanta • London • Vancouver

To the Grace Chapel family of Lexington, Massachusetts, my brothers and sisters, my co-laborers, my friends. Much of what this book is about, I learned from all of you. I love you.

1st printing, Moody Press; 2nd Printing, Thomas Nelson, Inc., Publishers, Nashville, Tennessee.

Published in Nashville, Tennessee, by Thomas Nelson, Inc., Publishers, and distributed in Canada by Word Communications, Ltd., Richmond, British Columbia.

Except where otherwise indicated, all Scripture quotations in this book are from the *New American Standard Bible*, ©1960, 1962, 1963, 1968, 1971, 1972, 1973, 1975, and 1977 by the Lockman Foundation, and are used by permission.

Scripture quotations marked TLB are from *The Living Bible* (Wheaton, Illinois: Tyndale House Publishers, 1971) and are used by permission.

Printed in the United States of America

Library of Congress Cataloging-in-Publication Data

MacDonald, Gordon.
    Ordering your private world / by Gordon MacDonald. — Expanded ed., anniversary ed.
      p. cm.
    Originally published: Nashville : Oliver-Nelson, c1985.
    ISBN 0-7852-7602-5 (pbk.)   ISBN 1-880828-94-4
    1. Christian life. I. Title.
BV4501.2.M227   1995
248.4—dc20

                                                95-23079
                                                CIP

37 38 39 40 — 01 00 99 98 97 96

Contents

Foreword

When 36 of us formed an experimental cell church in 1970, we envisioned a body of Christ that would edify one another through life in cell groups. We named it *The People Who Care*. It looked good—on paper!

One year to the day after its launch, we were hopelessly divided. Many were threatened by responsibility to and for others. The little group was far from ready to live in a community of love; inner values conflicted with wholehearted life in a cell church. I, too, lacked the restructuring of my own private world to lead the group. I resigned in despair.

Four months later, over half the members left the church to return to a traditional one and the remnant asked me to join them. In January, 1971, I suggested we close the formal membership for a period of six months and ask, "Who are we? How can we be effective if our inner worlds are in turmoil? How do we live by Kingdom values?"

God took us on a journey that changed us forever. Our values had been collected like germs off a street, and were often in conflict with Kingdom life. With the others, I began to seek for the inner cement I lacked, causing me to give up too soon on our experiment.

What Gordon MacDonald writes about in this book parallels the journey each one of us had to take. It was made more significant because we did it together! Six months later, we began to emerge from our journey as strong-hearted servants of God. Many tears were shed as we reorganized not *circumstances* but *inner-stances*.

As you enter your life of a cell leader, the chapters of this book and the cell leader's journal which follows it will seek to prepare you *within* for your ministry. If you are married, it would be valuable for your spouse to take the journey with you. Are you ready? Shall we begin?

Dr. Ralph W. Neighbour, Jr.

Touch Outreach Ministries

Preface:
Memo to the Disorganized

"I'm so disorganized!"
"I can't get my act together!"
"My inner life is a mess!"
"My private life is a failure!"

I have heard words like these scores of times. In conversations over breakfast, in the study where I meet people in my capacity as a pastor, in the living room of my home.

The words do not always come from people whose lives are falling apart or who are on the verge of some disaster, either. They may be said by men or women who appear to be extremely productive and successful. The first few times I heard self-disclosures like these, I was shocked. Now, many years later, I know for a fact that personal organization is a universal human struggle.

In Western culture we produce huge numbers of books to help us organize our work, our calendars, our production schedules, our studies, and our careers. I have not seen much that speaks directly to the question of internal, or spiritual, organization. And that is where the problem is most acute.

The successful people I have met who are concerned about disorganization are usually talking about the private dimension of their lives. They usually have the public dimension quite well regulated. It's this private part of life where we know ourselves best of all: this is where self-esteem is forged, where basic decisions about motives, values, and commit-

7

ments are made, where we commune with our God. I call it *the private world*, and I like to refer to its ideal state as one of *order*.

I know something about the disorganization of the private world because, like many others, I have struggled with it all my life. And to bring order to my private world has been one of my greatest battles.

Because I have lived in the context of the Christian gospel my entire life, Jesus Christ has never been a stranger to me. That does not mean, however, that I have always understood His lordship. Even though I have usually followed Him, I have too often followed from afar.

To understand what He meant when He spoke of "abiding in me" and my "abiding in Him" was very difficult, for I am one of many who has not easily taken to commitment. It has not been a simple thing for me to perceive the process and the purposes by which Christ wants to "abide" (John 15:4) in my private world. Frankly, I was often frustrated when I saw people who found this matter of "abiding" to be a perfectly comprehensible matter and who appeared to make it work.

Slowly and sometimes painfully, I have discovered that to bring organization to the private world where Christ chooses to live is both a lifelong and a daily matter. Something within—the Bible calls it sin—resists both His residence and all of the resulting order. It prefers a disorder where wrong motives and values can be hidden away and drawn to the surface in unguarded moments.

This disorder is a matter of daily concern. When I was a child living in a home where our bedrooms were not carpeted, I was often fascinated by the dustballs that collected under my bed. It was a mystery to me as to where they came from. It seemed as if some mysterious force came during the night and littered the floor with those dustballs while I slept. Today I find dustballs in my private world every day. How they got there, I am not sure. But I have to keep ahead of them in the daily discipline of bringing order into my inner sphere.

Let me be perfectly clear that I base this entire treatment of order in one's private world on the principle of the indwelling Christ, who mysteriously but definitely enters our lives upon our personal invitation and commitment. Apart from the center point of personal choice to follow Him, most of the words in this book will disintegrate into meaninglessness. *To bring order to one's personal life is to invite His control over every segment of one's life.*

For me, the pursuit of internal organization has been a lonely struggle because, frankly, I have found there is almost a universal reluctance to be candid and practical about these affairs. Much preaching on these matters is done in lofty terms that leave the hearer moved emotionally but unable to move specifically. More than once I have read a book or listened to a presentation on getting the spiritual life together, agreed with every word, and then realized that the proposed process was elusive and indefinite. It has been a struggle for people like me who want definite, measurable ways of responding to Christ's offer to live within us.

Even though the struggle has been mostly a lonely one, there has been assistance when I needed it. Naturally, there has been help from Scripture and the teachings I have received within the Christian tradition. Encouragement has come from my wife, Gail (whose private world is remarkably well ordered), from a number of mentors who have surrounded me from my earliest years, and from a host of men and women whom I will never meet in this life because they are dead. But I have encountered them in their biographies, and I have been delighted to discover that many of them also wrestled with the challenge of ordering their private worlds.

When I started making some public remarks about the order of my private world, I was impressed with how many people immediately reacted: pastors, lay people, men and women in various positions of leadership. "Your struggle is my struggle," they would say. "Give me any tips you can."

The private world can be divided into five sectors. The first deals with what makes us function as we do—our motivation. Are we *driven* people, propelled by the winds of our times, pressed to conform or compete? Or are we *called* people, the recipients of the gracious beckoning of Christ when He promises to make us into something?

Another sector of our private world centers on what we do

with the limited amount of time we have in this life. How we allocate time for the purposes of personal growth and service to others is a key to our health as persons. The third sector is intellectual: what are we doing with our minds, that remarkable part of us capable of receiving and processing the truth about creation?

The fourth sector of our private world, I would suggest, is that of the spirit. I am not concerned about being particularly theological with my vocabulary when I suggest there is a special, intimate place where we commune with the Father in a way that no one else can appreciate or understand. This place of the spirit I call the garden of our private world.

Finally, within us is a sector that draws us to rest, to a Sabbath peace. This peace is different from the amusement found so often in the visible world about us. And it is so significant that I believe it should be recognized as a uniquely essential source of inner organization.

Among the many biographies I have studied is one on Charles Cowman, missionary pioneer in Japan and Korea. His life was a remarkable testimony to the nature of commitment and its personal cost. In his later years his health broke, and he was forced into early retirement. The fact that he could no longer actively preach and direct the work of his fellowship missionaries was a terrible burden. One of his friends said this of him:

> Nothing impressed me more than Brother Cowman's quiet spirit. I never saw him ruffled, although at times I saw him wounded until the tears fell silently over his cheeks. He was a sensitive, tender spirit, but his secret cross became his crown.[1]

Cowman was a man with a private world in order. Not only was his life organized in its public dimension, it was organized within.

That is what this book is all about. I will not hesitate to be as practical as I know how. I will talk a lot about my own personal experiences, not because I consider myself a worthy

1. Lettie B. Cowman, *Charles E. Cowman* (Los Angeles: Oriental Missionary Society, 1928), p. 175.

model of internal order, but because I see myself as a fellow-struggler with all those for whom this issue is important.

Where possible, I have reached into the Bible for stories and supporting insights. But I must add that I have not over-indulged in theological argument. I have written with the assumption that the person eager to maintain order in the private world has already taken the step of choosing to live in obedience to God. And I have also assumed a basic understanding and agreement with the Christian way of life.

If you, the reader, find points of agreement with my treatment of this subject, then you may conclude as I have that much of the way we are teaching and preaching to one another these days may be seriously out of tune with spiritual reality. For I believe that some of the issues I have tried to unfold in the following pages are where life really simmers. Frankly, I do not think we hear enough about these issues. And I would be delighted if some of these thoughts, which come from my heart and are borrowed from other thinkers and writers, begin a dialogue among a few curious people.

Few authors write books alone. I certainly do not. In putting together my thoughts, I had not only the assistance of scores of authors who stimulated my thinking, but also the close and careful assistance of my wife, Gail, God's special gift to me, who read through version after version of these chapters, made innumerable comments in margins, and made me seek a greater level of realism and practicality.

To all those who think there is a more organized way to live within: join me on this bit of reflective adventure. At the end there may just be an opportunity for a deeper experience with God and an understanding of our mission in serving Him.

Memo to the Disorganized:

If my private world is in order, it will be because I am convinced that the inner world of the spiritual must govern the outer world of activity.

1
The Sinkhole Syndrome

The residents of a Florida apartment building awoke to a terrifying sight outside their windows. The ground beneath the street in front of their building had literally collapsed, creating a massive depression that Floridians call a sinkhole. Tumbling into the ever-deepening pit were automobiles, pavement, sidewalks, and lawn furniture. The building itself would obviously be the next to go.

Sinkholes occur, scientists say, when underground streams drain away during seasons of drought, causing the ground at the surface to lose its underlying support. Suddenly everything simply caves in, leaving people with a frightening suspicion that nothing—not even the earth beneath their feet—is trustworthy.

There are many people whose lives are like one of Florida's sinkholes. It is likely that at one time or another many of us have perceived ourselves to be on the verge of a sinkhole-like cave-in. In the feelings of numbing fatigue, a taste of apparent failure, or the bitter experience of disillusionment about goals or purposes, we may have sensed something within us about to give way. We feel we are just a moment from a collapse that will threaten to sweep our entire world into a bottomless pit. Sometimes there seems to be little that can be done to prevent such a collapse. What is wrong?

If we think about it for very long, we may discover the existence of an inner space—our private world—about which we were formerly ignorant. I hope it will become apparent that if neglected this private world will not sustain the weight of events and pressures that press upon it.

Some people are surprised and disturbed when they make such a self-discovery. They suddenly realize they have spent the majority of their time and energy establishing life on the visible level, at the surface. They have accumulated a host of good and perhaps even excellent assets such as academic degrees, work experience, key relationships, and physical strength or beauty.

There is nothing wrong with all of that. But often it is discovered almost too late that the private world of the person is in a state of disorderliness or weakness. And when that is true there is always potential for the sinkhole syndrome.

We must come to see ourselves as living in two very different worlds. Our outer, or public, world is easier to deal with. It is much more measurable, visible, and expandable. Our outer world consists of work, play, possessions, and a host of acquaintances that make up a social network. It is the part of our existence easiest to evaluate in terms of success, popularity, wealth, and beauty. But our inner world is more spiritual in nature. Here is a center in which choices and values can be determined, where solitude and reflection might be pursued. It is a place for conducting worship and confession, a quiet spot where the moral and spiritual pollution of the times need not penetrate.

The majority of us have been taught to manage our public worlds well. Of course, there will always be the undependable worker, the poorly organized homemaker, and the person whose social capacities are so immature that he becomes a drain on everyone around him. But most of us have learned to take orders, make schedules, and give directions. We know which systems best suit us in terms of work and relationship. We choose proper forms of leisure and pleasure. We have the capability to choose friends and make those relationships work well.

Our public worlds are filled with a seeming infinity of demands upon our time, our loyalties, our money, and our energies. And because these public worlds of ours are so visible, so real, we have to struggle to ignore all their seductions and demands. They scream for our attention and action.

The result is that our private world is often cheated, neglected because it does not shout quite so loudly. It can be effectively ignored for large periods of time before it gives way to a sinkhole-like cave-in.

The author Oscar Wilde was one who paid scant attention to his private world. William Barclay quotes Wilde's confession:

> The gods had given me almost everything. But I let myself be lured into long spells of senseless and sensual ease . . . Tired of being on the heights, I deliberately went to the depths in search for new sensation. What the paradox was to me in the sphere of thought, perversity became to me in the sphere of passion. I grew careless of the lives of others. I took pleasure where it pleased me, and passed on. I forgot that every little action of the common day makes or unmakes character, and that therefore what one has done in the secret chamber, one has some day to cry aloud from the house-top. I ceased to be lord over myself. I was no longer the captain of my soul, and did not know it. I allowed pleasure to dominate me. I ended in horrible disgrace.[1]

When Wilde writes, "I was no longer the captain of my soul," he describes a person whose inner world is in shambles, whose life is caving in. Although his words reach great heights of personal drama, they are similar to what many could say—many who, like him, have ignored their internal existence.

I believe that one of the great battlegrounds of our age is the private world of the individual. There is a contest that must be fought particularly by those who call themselves practicing Christians. Among them are those who work hard, shouldering massive responsibilities at home, at work, and at church. *They are good people, but they are very, very tired!* And thus they too often live on the verge of a sinkhole-like collapse. Why? Because although their worthwhile actions are very unlike those of Wilde, like him they become too public-

---

1. William Barclay, *The Letters to the Galatians and Ephesians* (Philadelphia: Westminster, 1976), p. 100.

world-oriented, ignoring the private side until it is almost too late.

Our Western cultural values have helped to blind us to this tendency. We are naively inclined to believe that the most publicly active person is also the most privately spiritual. We assume that the larger the church, the greater its heavenly blessing. The more information about the Bible a person possesses, we think, the closer he must be to God.

Because we tend to think like this, there is the temptation to give imbalanced attention to our public worlds at the expense of the private. More programs, more meetings, more learning experiences, more relationships, more busyness; until it all becomes so heavy at the surface of life that the whole thing trembles on the verge of collapse. Fatigue, disillusionment, failure, defeat all become frightening possibilities. The neglected private world can no longer hold the weight.

A man who has claimed Christian faith for more than ten years recently joined me on the sidelines of a soccer game in which our sons were playing. At halftime we took a stroll and inquired about each other. I asked him one of those questions that Christians ought to ask each other but feel odd in doing so.

I said, "Tell me how you're doing spiritually."

And he responded, "Interesting question! What's a good answer? Oh, I'm OK, I guess. I wish I could say I was growing or feeling closer to God. But the truth is that I'm sort of standing still."

I do not think I was out of line to pursue the matter because he gave me the impression he was genuinely interested in talking about this.

"Are you taking time regularly to order your inner life?"

He looked at me inquisitively. If I had said, "How's your quiet time?" he would have known exactly how to answer. That would have been measurable, and he could have responded in terms of days, hours and minutes, systems and techniques. But I had asked about the order of his inner life. And the key word is *order*, a word of *quality*, not quantity. And when he sensed that he showed discomfort.

"When does a guy ever get to order his inner life?" he

asked. "I've got work piled up to keep me going for the rest of the year. I'm out every night this week. My wife is after me to take a week's vacation. The house needs painting. So there's not too much time to think about ordering the inner life, as you put it."

He paused for a moment and then asked, *"What is the inner life anyway?"*

Suddenly I became aware that here was a professing Christian who had moved for years in Christian circles, had gained a Christian reputation for doing Christian things, but had never realized that underneath all the action and well-meaning noise there has got to be something solid, something dependable. That he saw himself as too busy to maintain an inner world, and that he was not sure he knew what it is anyway told me that he may have missed by a significant distance the central point of a life in touch with God. We had a lot to talk about.

Few people have had to wrestle with the pressures of a public world more than Anne Morrow Lindbergh, wife of the famous aviator. And she so jealously guarded her private world and wrote some insightful comments about it in her book *The Gift from the Sea:*

> I want first of all . . . to be at peace with myself. I want a singleness of eye, a purity of intention, a central core to my life that will enable me to carry out these obligations and activities as well as I can. I want, in fact—to borrow from the language of the saints—to live "in grace" as much of the time as possible. I am not using this term in a strictly theological sense. By grace I mean an inner harmony, essentially spiritual, which can be translated into outward harmony. I am seeking perhaps what Socrates asked for in the prayer from the Phaedrus when he said, "May the outward and inward man be one." I would like to achieve a state of inner spiritual grace from which I could function and give as I was meant to in the eye of God.[2]

Fred Mitchell, a leader in world missions, used to keep a motto on his desk that read, "Beware of the Barrenness of a

---

2. Anne Morrow Lindbergh, *The Gift from the Sea* (New York: Pantheon, 1955), pp. 23–24.

Busy Life." He too understood the potential collapse that follows when the inner world is ignored.

The Florida sinkhole is a physical picture of a spiritual problem with which many Western Christians must deal. As the pressure of life grows in the decades of the eighties and nineties, there will be more people whose lives resemble a sinkhole, unless they gaze inward and ask themselves, Is there a private world beneath the noise and action at the surface? A world that needs to be explored and maintained? Can strength and resilience be developed that will bear up under the pressure at the surface?

In a lonely moment in Washington when John Quincy Adams was overwhelmed by homesickness for his Massachusetts family, he wrote them a letter, addressing comments of encouragement and counsel to each son and daughter. To his daughter he wrote about the prospect of marriage and the kind of man she should choose to marry. His words reveal how highly he regarded an ordered private world:

> Daughter! Get you an honest man for a husband and keep him honest. No matter whether he is rich, provided he be independent. Regard the honor and moral character of the man, more than all other circumstances. *Think of no other greatness but that of the soul, no other riches but those of the heart.*(Italics added)[3]

---

3. Dorothie Bobbe, *Abigail Adams* (New York: Putnam, 1966), p. 206.

Memo to the Disorganized:

If my private world is in order, it will be because I make a daily choice to monitor its state of orderliness.

2

The View from the Bridge

A close friend was once an officer aboard a United States Navy nuclear submarine. He related to me an experience that happened one day while the sub was on duty in the Mediterranean. Many ships were passing overhead on the surface, and the submarine was having to make a large number of violent maneuvers to avoid possible collisions.

In the absence of the captain, my friend was duty officer, in charge of giving the commands by which the submarine was positioned at each moment. Because there was such a sudden and unusual amount of movement, the captain, who had been in his own quarters, suddenly appeared on the bridge asking, "Is everything all right?"

"Yes, sir!" was my friend's reply.

The captain took a quick look around and then started back out through the hatch to leave the bridge. As he disappeared he said, "It looks all right to me too."

That simple, routine encounter between a naval commander and one of his trusted officers provided me with a helpful picture of the order of one's private world. All around that submarine potential danger of collision was lurking. It was enough to make any alert captain show concern. But that danger was outside. Down deep inside the sub was a quiet place where there could be absolute control of the ship's destiny. And that was where the captain instinctively headed.

In that center of command there was not an ounce of panic; only a calm and deliberate series of actions being carried on by a highly trained crew of seamen doing their job. Thus when the commander appeared on the bridge to assure himself that everything was in order, it was. "Is everything all right?" he asked. Assured that it was, he looked about and agreed, "It looks all right to me too." He had gone to the right place and received the proper answer.

That is how the captain organized his sub. The appropriate procedures were practiced a thousand times when there was no danger. Thus, when it was time for action in a precarious situation, there was no need for the captain to panic. He could anticipate an excellent performance from the people on the bridge. When things are in order there, the submarine is secure no matter what the external circumstances. "It looks good to me too," says the captain.

But there have been cases in which those procedures have been ignored, perhaps left unpracticed. Then there can be disaster. Ships collide and sink, causing great loss. And so it is with human life when there is disorganization on the "bridge" of the inner world. The accidents that occur there have names like *burnout, breakdown*, or *blow-up*.

It is one thing for a person to make a mistake, or even to fail. We learn our best lessons of procedure and character under such conditions. But it is another thing to watch human beings disintegrate before our very eyes because there were no resources of interior support in the midst of the pressure.

The *Wall Street Journal* presented a series of articles entitled "Executive's Crisis," and one story featured Jerald H. Maxwell, a young entrepreneur who founded a successful hi-tech company. For a while he was considered to be a managerial and financial genius. But just for a while. Then there was a disintegration, a sinkhole collapse.

The day is etched into Jerald H. Maxwell's memory. His family will never forget it, either. To them it is the day he started weeping in his room, the day his exuberant self-confidence ended and his depression began, the day his world—and theirs—came tumbling down.

Maxwell had been fired! Everything fell apart, and he had no ability to handle the situation. The *Journal* continued:

> For the first time in his life, Mr. Maxwell was a failure, and it shattered him. His feeling of defeat led to an emotional break-down, gnawed away at the bonds between Mr. Maxwell and his wife and four sons and pushed him to the brink . . . "When things fell apart, they felt so bad I was ashamed," Mr. Maxwell recalls. He pauses and sighs, then goes on: "It says in the Bible that all you have to do is ask and you will receive. Well, I asked for death many times."[1]

Most of us have not asked for death as Maxwell did. But most of us have experienced the same pressure from the outer world, crowding in upon us to such an extent that we wondered if some sort of death was not imminent. During such moments we ask ourselves about the strength of our reserves—whether or not we can keep on going, whether it is worth it to keep pressing, whether it may be time to "cut and run." In short, we are not sure that there is enough spiritual, psychic, or physical energy to keep moving at the pace we are presently trying to maintain.

The key to all of this is to do what the captain of that submarine did. When there was a sense of violent turbulence all around, he headed for the bridge to determine whether or not things were in order. The answer, he knew, would be found nowhere else. And if everything was all right there, he knew he could retire to his quarters with confidence. The ship could handle the turbulent circumstances if everything was all right on the bridge.

One of my favorite Bible stories tells of the afternoon the disciples found themselves in a raging storm on the Sea of Galilee. Soon they were terrified and had lost all of their composure. Here were men who had fished this sea for years, who had their own equipment, and who must have seen such storms before. But for some reason, this time they were not able to handle the situation. Jesus, on the other hand, was asleep in the rear of the boat, and they ran to Him, furious that He seemed not to care that loss of life was a real threat.

1. "Executive's Crisis," *Wall Street Journal*, 12 March 1982, p. 1.

Perhaps we should at least credit them with knowing where to run.

After Christ had pressed peace into the storm, He asked the question that was central to all of their personal growth and development as spiritual leaders: "Where is your faith?" He could have asked in language I have been using, "Why isn't the bridge of your private world in better order?"

Why is it that for so many the answer to personal tension and pressure lies not in going to the bridge of life but rather in attempting to run faster, protest more vigorously, accumulate more, collect more data, and gain more expertise? We are of an age in which it seems instinctive to give attention to every cubic inch of life other than our inner worlds—the only place from which we can gain the strength to brave, or even beat, any outer turbulence.

Biblical writers believed in the principle of going to the bridge; they knew and taught that the development and maintenance of our inner worlds should be our highest priority. That is one practical reason that their work has transcended all times and cultures. For what they wrote they received from the Creator *who made us to work most effectively from the inner world toward the outer.*

One writer of Proverbs put the principle of the inner world in these words:

"Watch over your heart with all diligence, for from it flow the springs of life" (Proverbs 4:23).

In one simple sentence the writer has conveyed to us a most amazing insight. What I call the "bridge," he calls the "heart." He sees the heart as a spring, and suggests that out of it can flow the energy, the insight, and the force that do not succumb to outer turbulence but rather overcome it. Keep the heart, he says, and it will become a wellspring of life from which you and others can drink.

But what does it mean to "keep" the heart? For one thing, the writer is obviously concerned that the heart be protected from influences outside itself that might jeopardize its integrity. The writer is also concerned about the strength and development of the heart in order to increase its capacity to bring order to one's life.

But even behind these possible lessons from the metaphor is the fact that keeping or guarding of the heart, the "bridge" of human life, is a deliberate and disciplined choice a man or woman must make. We must *choose* to keep the heart. Its health and productivity cannot be assumed; it must be constantly protected and maintained. Again, we need to remember what the captain of the submarine did when he felt something out of the ordinary going on: he immediately headed for the bridge. Why? Because he knew that that was the place in which all capability to face danger would be found.

In the New Testament, Paul made the same sort of observation when he challenged Christians to "not be conformed to this [outer] world, but be transformed by the renewing of your mind" (Romans 12:2).

J. B. Phillips translated Paul's words like this: "Don't let the world squeeze you into its mold."

The apostle set forth an ageless truth. He was directing that a right choice be made. Are we going to order our inner worlds so that they will create influence on the outer world? Or will we neglect our private worlds and thus permit the outer sphere to shape us? This is a choice we have to make every day of our lives.

This is an incredible thought. And it is the sort of insight that the terminated executive in the *Wall Street Journal* article had ignored. The evidence? His cave-in, when the world about him faced him with crushing pressure. He had no reserve of inner strength, no order to his private world.

Mary Slessor was a young single woman who left Scotland at the turn of the century to go to a part of Africa that was infested with disease and indescribable danger. But she had an indomitable spirit and kept going when lesser men and women broke down, ran, and never came back. Once, after a particularly draining day, she found herself trying to sleep in a crude jungle hut. Of that night she wrote:

> I am not very particular about my bed these days, but as I lay on a few dirty sticks laid across and covered with a litter of dirty

corn-shells, with plenty of rats and insects, three women and an infant three days old alongside, and over a dozen sheep and goats and cows outside, you don't wonder that I slept little. *But I had such a comfortable quiet night in my own heart.* (Italics added)[2]

Now that is the sort of thing we are thinking about when we address the question of order in our private world. Whether you call it the "bridge" in naval language or the "heart" in biblical language, the point is the same: there must be a quiet place where all is in order, a place from which comes the energy that overcomes turbulence and is not intimidated by it.

We will know that we have learned this significant principle when we come to the point where the development and maintenance of a strong inner world becomes the most important single function of our existence. Then in the moment when pressure rises and tension increases, we can ask, "Is everything all right?" And discovering that it is, we can say with the heart, "It looks all right to me, too."

2. James Buchan, *The Indomitable Mary Slessor* (New York: Seabury, 1981), p. 86.

Sector One

Memo to the Disorganized:

If my private world is in order, it will be because I recognize my proneness to operate according to schemes and patterns not made of God but fashioned by a disordered past.

3

Caught in a Golden Cage

The twelve men who followed Jesus Christ and ultimately founded His church were a strange group. There is not one of them (with the possible exception of John, whom I find to be likable and nonthreatening) I would have picked to lead a movement of the proportions of Christ's mission. No, I would not have picked them. But Jesus called them, and you know the result.

Frankly, some of those volunteers who were turned down by Jesus are more my style. They were go-getters; they knew a good thing when they saw it. They seem to have been bursting with enthusiasm. And He turned them down! Why?

Perhaps Jesus, with His extraordinary insight, looked into their private worlds and saw danger signs. Perhaps He saw *driven men*, out to make something of themselves. Maybe the very thing I like about them was the problem: they wanted to control the situation by saying when they would start and where they would go.

Perhaps (it's pure speculation) if they had come aboard we would have discovered that they had a lot more in their agendas than was apparent at first. We would have found that they were men with their own plans and schemes, goals and objectives. And Jesus Christ will not do mighty works in the private worlds of people who are so driven. He never has. He seems to prefer to work with people whom He calls. And that is why the Bible knows nothing of volunteers, only the called.

In an exploration of the inner sphere of the person, one has to begin somewhere, and I have chosen to begin where Christ appears to have begun—with the distinction between the *called* and the *driven*. Somehow He separated people out on the basis of their tendency to be driven or their willingness to be called. He dealt with their motives, the basis of their spiritual energy, and the sorts of gratification in which they were interested. He called those who were drawn to Him and avoided those who were driven and wanted to use Him.

How can you spot a driven person? Today it is relatively easy. Driven people show the marks of stress. Look for symptoms of stress, and you have probably found some driven men and women.

The contemporary world is giving a lot of attention to the subject of stress. Stress is a topic for books, for research, and the doctor's examination room virtually every time someone feels chest pains or stomach upset. Many people commit entire careers to its study. Scientists measure stress in laboratories by subjecting various materials to all sorts of pressure and temperature and vibration. Engineers monitor it in the frames and engines of automobiles and airplanes by driving or flying them under extreme conditions for thousands of miles. Stress in human beings is closely checked while people fly through space, sit in a pressure chamber at the bottom of the ocean, or face medical tests in a hospital examination lab. A man I know has developed a sensitive measuring device that traces brain waves and can tell the researcher the minute the subject of his study is over-stressed.

In the past decade it has become very apparent that many people in our society are under constant and destructive stress, as life for them reaches a pace that offers little time for any restorative rest and retreat. *Time* magazine reported:

In the past 30 years, doctors and health officials have come to realize how heavy a toll stress is taking on the nation's well-being. According to the American Academy of Family Physicians, two-thirds of office visits to family doctors are prompted by stress-related symptoms. At the same time, leaders of industry have become alarmed by the huge cost of such symptoms in absenteeism, company medical expenses and lost productivity.[1]

The article went on to say that the effects of stress are costing American business $50 to $75 billion a year, or more than $750 for every U.S. worker. Stress, *Time* says, "is a major contributor, either directly or indirectly, to coronary heart disease, cancer, lung ailments, accidental injuries, cirrhosis of the liver and suicide." And that is just the beginning.

What is behind all this? *Time* quotes Dr. Joel Elkes of the University of Louisville: "Our mode of life itself, the way we live, is emerging as today's principal cause of illness."

We are all aware that there is a kind of stress that is beneficial because it brings out the best in performers, athletes, or executives. But most of the attention presently being given to the subject centers on the kinds of stress that diminish human capacity rather than enhance it.

One fascinating study on stress has been conducted by Dr. Thomas Holmes. Holmes is known for his development of the famous Social Readjustment Rating Scale, or, as most of us know it, the Holmes Stress Chart. Holmes's stress chart is a simple measurement device that indicates how much pressure a person is probably facing and how close he may be to dangerous physical and psychic consequences.

After considerable research, various events common to all of us were assigned point totals by Holmes and his associates. Each point was called a "life-change unit." An accumulation of more than 200 of these units in any one year, Holmes suggests, could be the warning of a potential heart attack, emotional stress, or breakdown of the ability to function as a healthy person. The death of a spouse, for example, commands the highest number of "life-change" units, 100. Being fired from a job produces 47 points, while the acquisition of a new family member provides 39. Not all stress-producing events listed by Holmes are negative. Even positive and happy events such as Christmas (12 points) and vacations (13) create stress.

1. "Stress: Can We Cope?" *Time*, 6 June 1983, pp. 48–54.

My experience is that it is not unusual to talk with people whose point total is well beyond 200. A pastor, for example, comes to visit with me at my office. His point total, he tells me, is 324. His blood pressure is dangerously high; he suffers from constant stomach pains, he fears an ulcer, and he does not sleep well at night. On another day, I sit at breakfast with a young executive who admits that until recently his ambition had been to accumulate a million dollars before the age of 35. When he matches his present situation up against the Holmes Stress Chart, he is horrified to discover that his point total is 412. What do these two men from the business and religious world have in common?

These are what I call *driven* men. And their drive is costing them terribly—the point totals are simply a numerical indication of that fact. I use the word *driven* because it describes not only the condition in which they are pursuing life, but also because it is descriptive of the way many of the rest of us are not facing up to the reality of what we are doing to ourselves. Perhaps we are being driven toward goals and objectives without always understanding why. Or we may not be aware of the real cost to our minds, our bodies, and, of course, our hearts. By *heart* I mean the one written about in Proverbs 4:23, that fountainhead from which comes the energy of life.

There are lots of driven people doing very good things. Driven people are not necessarily bad folk, although the consequences of their drivenness may produce unfortunate results. In fact, driven people often make great contributions. They start organizations; they provide jobs and opportunities; they are often very bright and offer ways and means of doing things that benefit many other people. But nevertheless they are driven, and one worries about their ability to sustain the pace without danger to themselves.

Can driven people be spotted? Yes, of course. There are many symptoms that suggest a person is driven. Among the ones I see most often are these:

(1) *A driven person is most often gratified only by accomplishment.* Somewhere in the process of maturation this person discovers that the only way he can feel good about himself and his world is to accumulate accomplishments. This discov-

ery may be the result of formative influences at an early age; as a child, affirmation and approval may have been received from a parent or influential mentor only when something had been finished. Nothing of value may have ever been said until that task was completed. Thus the only way he could find love and acceptance was through accomplishment.

A psychology of achievement sometimes captures the heart in circumstances like that. A person begins to reason that if one accomplishment resulted in good feelings and the praise of others, then several more accomplishments may bring an abundance of good feelings and affirmations.

So the driven person begins to look for ways to accumulate more and more achievements. He will soon be found doing two or three things at one time, because that brings even more of this strange sort of pleasure. He becomes the sort of person who is always reading books and attending seminars that promise to help him to use what time he has even more effectively. Why? So that he can produce more accomplishments, which in turn will provide greater gratification.

This is the kind of person who sees life only in terms of results. As such he has little appreciation for the *process* leading toward results. This kind of person would love to fly from New York to Los Angeles at supersonic speed because to travel at ground speed and see the hills of Pennsylvania, the golden wheat of Iowa and Nebraska, the awesomeness of the Rockies, and the deserts of Utah and Nevada would be a terrible waste of time. Upon arrival in Los Angeles after a swift two-hour trip, this driven person would be highly irritated if the plane took four extra minutes to get into the gate. Arrival is everything to this accomplishment-oriented individual; the trip means nothing.

(2) *A driven person is preoccupied with the symbols of accomplishment.* He is usually conscious of the concept of power, and he seeks to possess it in order to wield it. That means that he will be aware of the symbols of status: titles, office size and location, positions on organizational charts, and special privileges.

There is generally a concern for one's own notoriety when in a state of drivenness. Who, the driven person wonders, knows about what I am doing? How can I be better connected with the "greats" of my world? These questions often preoccupy the driven person.

(3) *A driven person is usually caught in the uncontrolled pursuit of expansion.* Driven people like to be a part of something that is getting bigger and more successful. They are usually on the move, seeking the biggest and the best opportunities. They rarely have any time to appreciate the achievements to date.

The nineteenth-century English preacher Charles Spurgeon once said:

> Success exposes a man to the pressures of people and thus tempts him to hold on to his gains by means of fleshly methods and practices, and to let himself be ruled wholly by the dictatorial demands of incessant expansion. Success can go to my head and will unless I remember that it is God who accomplishes the work, that he can continue to do so without my help, and that he will be able to make out with other means whenever he wants to cut me out.[2]

You can see this unfortunate principle in the pursuit of some careers. But you can also see it in the context of spiritual activity, for there is such a thing as a spiritually driven person who is never satisfied with who he is or what he accomplishes in religious work. And of course this means that his attitude toward those around him is much the same. He is rarely pleased with the progress of his peers or subordinates. He lives in a constant state of uneasiness and restlessness, looking for more efficient methods, greater results, deeper spiritual experiences. There is usually no sign that he will ever be satisfied with himself or anyone else.

(4) *Driven people tend to have a limited regard for integrity.* They can become so preoccupied with success and achievement that they have little time to stop and ask if their inner person is keeping pace with the outer process. Usually it is not, and there is an increasing gap, a breakdown in integrity. People like this often become progressively deceitful; and they not only deceive others, they deceive themselves. In the at-

2. Cited in J. Oswald Sanders, *Spiritual Leadership* (Chicago: Moody, 1967), p. 23.

tempt to push ahead relentlessly, they lie to themselves about motives; values and morals are compromised. Shortcuts to success become a way of life. Because the goal is so important, they drift into ethical shabbiness. Driven people become frighteningly pragmatic.

(5) *Driven people often possess limited or undeveloped people skills.* They are not noted for getting along well with others. They were not born without the capacity to get along with others, but projects are more important to them than people. Because their eyes are upon goals and objectives, they rarely take note of the people about them, unless they can be used for the fulfillment of one of the goals. And if others are not found to be useful, then they may be seen as obstacles or competitors when it comes to getting something done.

There is usually a "trail of bodies" in the wake of the driven person. Where once others praised him for his seemingly great leadership, there soon appears a steady increase in frustration and hostility, as they see that the driven person cares very little about the health and growth of human beings. It becomes apparent that there is a non-negotiable agenda, and it is supreme above all other things. Colleagues and subordinates in the orbit of the driven person slowly drop away, one after another, exhausted, exploited, and disillusioned. Of this person we are most likely to find ourselves saying, "He is miserable to work with, but he certainly gets things done."

And therein lies the rub. He gets things done, but he may destroy people in the process. Not an attractive sight. Yet the ironic thing, which cannot be ignored, is that in almost every great organization, religious and secular, people of this sort can be found in key positions. Even though they carry with them the seeds of relational disaster, they often are indispensable to the action.

(6) *Driven people tend to be highly competitive.* They see each effort as a win-or-lose game. And, of course, the driven person feels he must win, must look good before others. The more driven he is, the larger the score by which he needs to win. Winning provides the evidence the driven person desperately needs that he is right, valuable, and important. Thus, he

is likely to see others as competitors or as enemies who must be beaten—perhaps even humiliated—in the process.

(7) *A driven person often possesses a volcanic force of anger,* which can erupt any time he senses opposition or disloyalty. This anger can be triggered when people disagree, offer an alternative solution to a problem, or even hint at just a bit of criticism.

The anger may not surface as physical violence. But it can take the form of verbal brutality: profanity or humiliating insults, for example. The anger can express itself in vindictive acts such as firing people, slandering them before peers, or simply denying them things they have come to expect, such as affection, money, or even companionship.

A close friend tells of sitting in an office with several working associates while the office manager, a woman who had worked for the company for fifteen years, made a plea for a week off to be with a sick baby. She made the mistake of responding tearfully when the boss refused her request. When he turned and saw her tears, he snarled, "Clean out your desk and get out of here; I don't need you anyhow." When she was gone he turned to the horrified onlookers and said, "Let's get one thing straight; you're all here for only one reason: to make me money. And if you don't like it, get out right now!"

Tragically, many good people who surround the driven person are more than willing to take the impact of such anger although it desperately hurts them, because they reason that the boss or the leader is getting things done, that he is being blessed by God, or that no one can argue with success. Sometimes the anger and its cruel effects are accepted simply because no one has either the courage or the ability to stand up to the driven person.

Recently a person who serves on the board of a major Christian organization told me of encounters with the executive director that included outbursts of anger studded with extraordinary profanity and demeaning language. When I asked why board members accepted this form of behavior, which was neither rare nor open to excuse, he said, "I guess we were so impressed with the way that God seemed to use him in his public ministry that we were reluctant to confront."

Is there anything else worth saying about the driven person, who by now appears to be entirely unlikeable? Yes, simply this:

(8) *Driven people are usually abnormally busy.* They are usually too busy for the pursuit of ordinary relationships in marriage, family, or friendship, or even to carry on a relationship with themselves—not to speak of one with God. Because driven people rarely think they have accomplished enough, they seize every available minute to attend more meetings, to study more material, to initiate more projects. They operate on the precept that a reputation for busyness is a sign of success and personal importance. Thus they attempt to impress people with the fullness of their schedule. They may even express a high level of self-pity, bemoaning the "trap" of responsibility they claim to be in, wishing aloud that there was some possible release from all that they have to live with. But just try to suggest a way out!

The truth is that the very worst thing that could happen to them would be if someone provided them with a way out. They really wouldn't know what to do with themselves if there were suddenly less to do. Busyness for the driven person becomes a habit, a way of life and thought. They find it enjoyable to complain and gather pity, and they would probably not want it any different. But tell a driven person that, and you'll make him angry.

This then is the driven person—not an entirely attractive picture. What often disturbs me as I look at this picture is the fact that much of our world is run by driven people. We have created a system that rides on their backs. And where that is true in businesses, in churches, and in homes, the growth of people is often sacrificed for accomplishment and accumulation.

Pastors who are driven men have been known to burn out scores of assistants and lay leaders because of their need to head organizations that are the biggest, the best, and the most well-known. There are business people who claim Christian faith and who have enjoyed a reputation for graciousness in the church, but who are ruthless in the office, pushing people and squeezing them for the last ounce of energy simply so that they themselves can enjoy the gratification of winning, accumulating, or establishing a reputation.

Recently a businessman became a Christian through the witness of a layman who is a good friend of mine. Not long after making his choice to follow Jesus Christ, he wrote a long letter to my friend who had guided him into faith. In it he described some of his struggles as the result of his driven condition. I requested permission to share part of the letter because it so vividly illustrated the driven person. He wrote:

Several years ago I was at a point of great frustration in my life. Although I had a wonderful wife and three beautiful sons, my career was going badly. I had few friends, my oldest son began getting into trouble—he started failing in school—I was suffering from depression, there was great tension and unhappiness in my family. At that time I had an opportunity to travel overseas where I stayed to work in a foreign company. This new opportunity was such an excellent one, financially and career-wise, that I made it number one in my life, forsaking all other values. I did many wrong (i.e., sinful) things to advance my position and success. I justified them as being of good consequence to my family (more money, etc.)—resulted in my lying to myself and my family and behaving wrongly in many ways.

Of course this was intolerable to my wife and she and my family returned to the U.S. I was still blind, however, to the problems that were within me. My success, my salary, my career—all moved upward. I *was caught in a golden cage* . . . [italics mine]

Although many wonderful things were happening outside me, inside I was losing everything. My capacity to reason and my capacity to decide were both weakened. I would evaluate alternatives constantly going over various options, always trying to pick the one that would maximize success and career. I knew in my heart that something was terribly wrong. I went to church, but the words there couldn't reach me. I was too caught up in my own world.

After a terrible episode with my family several weeks ago, I completely gave up my course of thinking and went to a hotel room for nine days to figure out what to do. The more I thought the more troubled I became. I began to realize how dead I really was, how so much of my life was dark. And worse than that, I could see no way out. My only solution was to run and hide, to start in a different place, to sever all connections.

This brutal description of a man on the bottom fortunately has a happy ending. For not long after his nine-day experience in a hotel room, he discovered the love of God and its capacity to engender dramatic change in his life. And a driven man turned into what we will call in our next chapter a *called man*. He got out of his golden cage.

In the Bible few men typify the driven man better than Saul, the first king of Israel. Unlike the previous story, which had a happy conclusion, this one has a miserable ending, for Saul never got out of his golden cage. All he did was heap increasing amounts of stress upon himself. And it destroyed him.

The Bible's introduction to Saul should be warning enough that the man had some flaws that, if not addressed within his inner world, would cause him quickly to lose personal control.

> There was a man of Benjamin whose name was Kish the son of Abiel, the son of Zeror, the son of Becorath, the son of Aphiah, the son of a Benjamite, a mighty man of valor. And he had a son whose name was Saul, a choice and handsome man, and there was not a more handsome person than he among the sons of Israel; from his shoulders and up he was taller than any of the people (1 Samuel 9:1–2).

Saul possessed three unearned characteristics at the beginning of his public life that had the potential to become assets or serious liabilities. Which they would be was his choice. And how Saul made those choices depended upon the daily order of his private world.

The three? First, wealth; second, an attractive appearance; and third, a physically large and well-developed body. All were attributes of a person's public world. In other words, the initial impression was that Saul was a better man than anyone around him. All three external marks commanded attention and gained him quick advantages. (Each time I think of Saul's natural gifts, I recall the bank president some years ago who said to me, "MacDonald, you could go a long way in the business world if you were about six inches taller.") And, most importantly, they provided him with a sort of charisma that made possible his achieving some early success without ever having to develop a heart of wisdom or spiritual stature. He was simply a fast starter.

As Saul's story unfolds in the biblical text we learn some other things about the man, things that could have either contributed to his success or become a part of his ultimate failure. We are told, for example, that he was good with words. When he was given a chance to speak before crowds, he was eloquent. The stage was set for a man to consolidate power and command recognition without ever having to develop any sense of a strong inner world first. And that was where the danger lay.

When Saul became king of Israel, he enjoyed too much immediate success. It apparently made him unaware that he had any limits to his life. He spent little time pondering his need for others, engendering a relationship with God, or even facing his responsibilities toward the people over whom he ruled. The signs of a driven man began to appear.

Saul became a busy man; he saw worlds he thought needed conquering. Thus when he faced an impending battle with the Philistines, Israel's great enemy of the day, and waited at Gilgal for Samuel the prophet to come and offer the necessary sacrifices, he grew impatient and irritable when the holy man did not arrive on time. Saul felt that his timetable was being compromised; he had to get on with things. His remedy? Offer the sacrifice himself. And that is exactly what he did.

The result? A rather serious breach of covenant with God. Offering sacrifice was the kind of thing prophets like Samuel did, not kings like Saul. But Saul had forgotten that because he saw himself as being too important.

From that time forward Saul found himself on a downhill track. "Now your kingdom shall not endure. The Lord has sought out for Himself a man after His own heart" (1 Samuel 13:14). This is how most driven men end.

Stripped of what blessing and assistance he had had from God up to this point, Saul's drivenness began to reveal itself even further. Soon all of his energies became consumed in holding onto his throne, competing with young David, who had caught the imagination of the people of Israel.

The Scriptures give several examples of Saul's explosive an-

ger, which drove him to outrage as well as to moments of para-
lyzing self-pity. By the end of his life, he was a man out of
control, seeing enemies behind every bush. Why? Because
from the very beginning Saul had been a driven man, and he
had never cultivated the order of his private world.

I wonder what Saul's point total would have been on Thomas
Holmes's stress chart. I suspect it would have been up in the
range of stroke and heart attack victims. But Saul never came
to grips with his drivenness, either through something like a
stress chart or by simply facing the inner rebukes God would
have liked for him to have heard within his private world. Saul
would not have lasted long among the twelve disciples Jesus
picked. His own compulsions were far too strong. That which
had driven him to grasp power and not let go, that which
had caused him to turn on his closest supporters, and that
which caused him to make a successive series of unwise decisions, finally led him to a humiliating death. He was the classic driven man.

To the extent that we see him in ourselves, we have work to
do in our private worlds. For an inner life fraught with unresolved drives will not be able to hear clearly the voice of
Christ when He calls. The noise and pain of stress will be too
great.

Unfortunately, our society abounds with Sauls, men and
women caught in golden cages, driven to accumulate, to be
recognized, or to achieve. Our churches, unfortunately,
abound with these driven people as well. Many churches are
fountains gone dry. Rather than being springs of life-giving
energy that cause people to grow and to delight in God's way,
they become sources of stress. The driven man's private world
is disordered. His cage may be lavishly golden. But it's a trap;
inside there is nothing that lasts.

Memo to the Disorganized:

If my private world is in order, it will be because, having faced up to what drives me, I listen quietly for the call of Christ.

4

The Tragic Tale
of a Successful Bum

When the couple came into my office for the first of a series of visits, they sat in chairs as far apart from one another as possible. It was obvious that neither liked the other, at least at the moment. And yet the agenda was the saving of a marriage—theirs.

She was asking him to leave the home, I was told. When I asked her why, she said it was the only possible way there would be any peace or normal life for the rest of the family. There was no infidelity, no single issue. She simply wasn't prepared to live with him for the rest of his life, given his temperament and value system.

But he didn't want to leave. In fact he was shocked that she should have come to this conclusion, he said. After all, he was a faithful provider; their home was quite large and located in an upper-class neighborhood. The kids had everything they wanted. It was hard to figure out, he went on, why she would want to end the marriage. Besides, weren't they Christians? He'd thought all along that Christians didn't believe in divorce or separation. Would I please solve their problem?

The story slowly emerged. It became clear that I was visiting with one of those driven men and his wife. His drivenness was costing a marriage, a family, and his physical health. That the marriage was virtually dead I could see in their body language. That the family was in ruins I could deduce from their descriptions of the attitudes of the children. That his health was in jeopardy was obvious when he told me of a bundle of ulcers, migraine headaches, and occasional chest pains. The story continued to unravel.

Because he owned his business, he had the freedom to work his own hours: nineteen to twenty per day. And because he had such responsibilities, he was rarely at any function important to his children. He usually left the home before anyone was out of bed in the morning, and he rarely came home until the youngest of the children was already back in bed for the night. If he was present at a family meal, he tended to be sullen and preoccupied. It was not a rare occurrence for him to be called to the phone in the middle of supper and remain there for the remainder of the hour solving some problem or closing a sale.

In conflict, he admitted, he was given to explosive anger; in relationships he could be abrasive and intimidating. Put into a social situation he was usually bored with conversation and tended to withdraw and drink too much. When asked who his friends were, he could name no one except business associates. And when challenged as to things of importance apart from his work, he could think only of his sports car, his boat, and his skybox season tickets to the Red Sox—things, not people, all of which, ironically, he was usually too busy to enjoy anyway.

This was a man with almost no order at all in his private world. Everything was external. His life was, by his own admission, a bundle of activity and accumulation. He could never do enough; he could never earn enough to be satisfied. Everything had to get bigger, better, and more impressive. What was driving him? Could there ever be order to his private world?

After several conversations I began to gain some insight into the fantastic energy source that drove this man into a way of life that was destroying everything around him. In the midst of one of our talks, I asked him about his father. Suddenly his mood became dramatically altered. Anyone could have sensed that I had abruptly uncovered a deeply sensitive matter.

What slowly unfolded was a tale of extreme relational pain. His father, I learned, was a man given to extreme sarcasm and ridicule. He had regularly told his son, "You're a bum; you will always be a bum, nothing better!" It had been said so many times that the words had become emblazoned as if on a neon sign in the center of this young man's private world.

Here was a man, now in his early forties, who had unconsciously made a lifelong commitment. He had committed himself to disproving the label given to him by his father. Somehow he would demonstrate with unimpeachable evidence *that he was not a bum*. It became the essential preoccupation of his life without his ever really knowing it.

Since a state of "un-bumness" was equated with hard work, high income, and the status of wealth, these things formed the cluster of objectives for this driven man. He would show that he was a hard worker by owning a business and making it the best in that section of the Yellow Pages. He would make sure that it produced large sums of money for him, even if some of the money was "dirtied" by the way it was obtained. The large house, the sports car, the season tickets among the finest boxes at Fenway would all be measurable disclaimers of the paternal charge of "bumness." And thus it was that my visitor became a driven man, driven to gain his father's respect and love.

Because his goals were all basically external, there was no need to cultivate an inner world. Relationships were not important; winning was. Spiritual health was not significant; physical strength was. Rest was not necessary; available time for more work was. And the accumulation of knowledge and wisdom was not a matter of value; sales technique and product innovation were.

He claimed that it was all part of his desire to provide for his family. Slowly we began to discover together that he was really trying to gain his father's affirmation and acceptance. He wanted to hear his father finally say, "Son, you're not a bum; I was entirely wrong."

What made this matter even stranger was that the unpleasable father had been dead for several years. Yet the son, now in midlife, continued to work to gain that approval. What had started as an objective became a habit of living he could not break.

WHY ARE PEOPLE DRIVEN?

Why do so many people appear to be driven? My friend is an extreme example of one reason. He typifies those who grew up in *environments where "well done" was never heard.* When such acceptance and affirmation is lacking, it is by no means unusual for the respect-starved person to conclude that more work, greater accumulation of symbols of success, or worldly praise will finally convince the significant person who has withheld approval to finally say, "Son (daughter), you are not a bum after all. I'm terribly proud to be your father."

Many people in leadership positions share this sort of background and this sort of insecurity. Some leaders appear to be highly benevolent people, doing good things, and are praised for dedicated, selfless actions; the fact may be that they are pushed toward the hope of gaining the acceptance and approval of just one significant person in their past. And if they cannot gain that, then they develop an insatiable appetite for applause, wealth, or power from other sources in an attempt to compensate for the loss. Rarely, however, is satisfaction reached. This is because their pursuit is in the public world; the private world is left empty and wanting. And that is where the real ache lies.

Another source of drivenness *is an early experience of serious deprivation or shame.* In his book *Creative Suffering* (New York: Harper & Row, 1983), Paul Tournier points out that an enormous number of world political leaders over the past several centuries have been orphans. Having grown up in a context of personal loss in terms of intimate parental love and emotional closeness, they may have sought a compensatory experience in the embrace of the crowds. Behind their great drive for power may be the simple need for love. Rather than meeting this need through the ordering of the private world within, they have chosen to pursue it on the external level.

Driven people can also come from backgrounds in which

there has been a sense of great shame or embarrassment. In his remarkably candid *The Man Who Could Do No Wrong* (Lincoln, Va.: Chosen Books, 1981), pastor Charles Blair describes his own childhood during the Depression days in Oklahoma. With pain he recalls his daily task of hauling the free government-issue milk from the local firehouse to home. As he carried the milk pail down the street, he had to endure what he felt was raw scorn from boys his own age. Out of the agony of such moments came the resolve that the day would come when he would never again carry a symbolic milk pail, which signified a feeling of worthlessness.

Blair tells the story of an unforgettable walk home from school in the company of a girl about whom he had strong feelings. Suddenly a boy with a shiny new bicycle came up beside them and offered the girl a ride. Without hesitation she hopped onto the back fender, leaving Blair behind as she and the other boy rode off together. The humiliation of that moment caused Blair to quietly resolve that someday *he* would have the equivalent of a shiny bicycle, that *he* would have the wherewithal to make impressions that would command the attentions and loyalties of others.

And those resolves burned their way into his life. They became a source of the drive that subsequently, by his own account, betrayed him. He would later need to own the most attractive automobile, lead the most beautiful and largest church, and wear the most stylish of men's fashions. These things would prove that he had made it out of the Oklahoma Depression. He was not worthless; he was not poor. He could prove it. Look!

Charles Blair was running from something, and that meant that he had to run toward something. Although his drive was clothed in all sorts of impressive spiritual motives, and although his ministry was remarkably effective, down at the center were unresolved hurts of the past. Because these hurts remained a point of disorder in his private world, they came back to haunt him. They affected his choices and values and blinded him to what was really happening at a crucial moment of his life. The result? Serious disaster. Failure, embarrassment, and public humiliation.

But it must be added that he rebounded. That alone suggests hope for the driven man. Charles Blair the *driven* man of earlier years, running from shame, is now a *called* man, and he deserves the admiration of his friends. I consider his book to be one of the most significant I have ever read. It ought to be required reading for any man or woman who is in leadership.

Finally, *some people are simply raised in an environment where drivenness is a way of life.* In a book called *Wealth Addiction,* Philip Slater details the backgrounds of several living billionaires. In almost every account there is indication that as children these billionaires made the accumulation of things and the conquest of people their amusement. There was little if any play for the purpose of pure fun or exercise. They only knew how to win, how to accumulate. It was what they saw their parents doing, and they assumed that it was the only way to live. Thus the drive to grow rich and powerful began in the earliest days.

To such people an ordered private world has little meaning. The only thing worth giving attention to is the public world, where things can be measured, admired, and used.

Of course, driven people come out of many other backgrounds, and these are but a few samples. But one thing is sure in all cases: driven people will never enjoy the tranquility of an ordered private world. Their prime targets are all external, material, and measurable. Nothing else seems real; nothing else makes much sense. And it all must be held onto, as it was with Saul, who found that power was more important than the integrity of a friendship with David.

Let us be sure we understand that when we speak of driven people, we are not merely thinking of a highly competitive business person or a professional athlete. We are considering something much more pervasive than "workaholism." Any of us can look within and suddenly discover that *drivenness is our way of life.* We can be driven toward a superior Christian reputation, toward a desire for some dramatic spiritual experience, or toward a form of leadership that is really more a quest for domination of people than servanthood. A homemaker can be a driven person; so can a student. A driven person can be any of us.

HOPE FOR THE DRIVEN PERSON

Can the driven person be changed? Most certainly. It begins when such a person faces up to the fact that he is operating according to drives and not calls. That discovery is usually made in the blinding, searching light of an encounter with Christ. As the twelve disciples discovered, an audience with Jesus over a period of time exposes all the roots and expressions of drivenness.

To deal with drivenness, one must begin to ruthlessly appraise one's own motives and values just as Peter was forced to do in his periodic confrontations with Jesus. The person seeking relief from drivenness will find it wise to listen to mentors and critics who speak Christ's words to us today.

He may have some humbling acts of renunciation, some disciplined gestures of surrender of things—things that are not necessarily bad, but that have been important for all the wrong reasons.

Perhaps the driven person will have to grant forgiveness to some of those who in the past never offered the proper kind of affection and affirmation. And all of that may just be the beginning.

Paul the apostle in his pre-Christian days was driven. As a driven man, he studied, he joined, he attained, he defended, and he was applauded. The pace at which he was operating shortly before his conversion was almost manic. He was driven toward some illusive goal, and, later, when he could look back at that life-style with all of its compulsions, he would say, "It was all worthless."

Paul was driven until Christ called him. One gets the feeling that when Paul fell to his knees before the Lord while on the road to Damascus, there was an explosion of relief within his private world. What a change from the drivenness that had pushed him toward Damascus in an attempt to stamp out Christianity to that dramatic moment when, in complete submission, he asked Jesus Christ, "What shall I do, Lord?" A driven man was converted into a called one.

I could have wished this for the man who came to talk with me about his wife's demand that he leave their house. Time after time we talked about his insatiable drive to win, to earn, to impress. There were a few occasions when I thought he was catching the message, when I allowed myself to be convinced we were making progress. I actually believed that he was going to move the center of his life from the public aspect of his world to the private side.

I could almost see him kneeling before Christ offering up his drivenness, being washed clean of all the old terribly painful memories of a father who had flung a sense of "bumness" into his private world. How much I wanted my friend, the successful bum, to see himself a disciple called by Christ, and not one driven to achieve in order to prove something.

But it never happened. And eventually we lost contact. The last I heard, his drivenness cost him everything: family, marriage, business. For it drove him right to his grave.

Memo to the Disorganized:

If my private world is in order, it will be because I see
myself as Christ's steward and not as master of my purpose, my role, and my identity.

5

Living as
a Called Person

In his book *A Casket of Cameos*, F. W. Boreham reflects on
the faith of Harriet Beecher Stowe's Uncle Tom. The old slave
had been wrenched from his old Kentucky home and put upon
a steamship headed for unknown places. It was a terrible moment of crisis, and, Boreham observes, "Uncle Tom's faith was
staggered. It really seemed to him that, in leaving Aunt Chloe
and the children and his old companions, he was leaving God!"

Falling asleep, the slave had a dream. "He dreamed that he
was back again, and that little Eva was reading to him from
the Bible as of old. He could hear her voice: 'When thou pass-
est through the waters, I will be with thee; for I am the Lord
thy God, the Holy One of Israel, Thy Saviour.'" Boreham continues:

A little later, poor Tom was writhing under the cruel lash of his
new owner. "But," says Mrs. Stowe, *"The blows fell only upon the
outer man, and not, as before, on the heart.* Tom stood sub-
missive; and yet Legree could not hide from himself the fact that
his power over his victim had gone. As Tom disappeared in his
cabin, and Legree wheeled his horse suddenly round, there
passed through the tyrant's mind one of those vivid flashes that
often send the lightning of conscience across the dark and wicked
soul. He understood full well that it was God who was standing
between him and Tom, and he blasphemed Him!" (Italics added)[1]

1. Frank W. Boreham, *A Casket of Cameos* (1924: reprint, Valley Forge,
Pa.: Judson, 1950), p. 266.

THE CALLED PERSON

It is this quality of certitude for which we seek when we compare *driven* persons and *called* persons. Driven people are confident they have that quality as they forge ahead. But often, at the moment when it is least expected, hostile events conspire, and there can be collapse. Called people have strength from within, perseverance and power that are impervious to the blows from without.

Called men and women can come from the strangest places and carry the most unique qualifications. They may be the unnoticed, the unappreciated, the unsophisticated. Look again at the men Christ picked: few if any of them would have been candidates for high positions in organized religion or big business. It is not that they were unusually awkward. It is just that they were among the ordinary. But Christ called them, and that made all the difference.

Rather than living according to drivenness, some are drawn toward the beckoning hand of the calling Father. Such calls are usually heard within an ordered private world.

JOHN—A PICTURE OF A CALLED MAN

John the Baptizer is a powerful example of a called man. He had the audacity to tell fellow Jews that they ought to quit justifying themselves on the basis of their sense of superior racial identity and face up to their need for spiritual and moral repentance. Baptism, he said, would testify to the genuineness of their contrition. No wonder no one was ever neutral about John. He never minced his words. He was a man one loved or hated; one of the latter type finally took off his head. But not until he finished his work.

John, the called man, is a remarkable contrast to Saul, the driven man. John seems to have had from the very beginning a vivid sense of destiny, the result of a heavenly assignment that came from deep within himself. One sees the contrast between Saul and John most vividly when their personal identities and their sense of vocational security are under attack. Saul, the driven man, you will remember, reacted violently, lashing out against his perceived enemies when he became convinced that the preservation of his power and the survival of his position relied solely upon himself.

But John is another story. Watch him when news comes that his popularity may be on the verge of serious decline. To be just a bit dramatic, let me suggest that John is facing the loss of his job. The account I have in mind opens after John has introduced Christ to the multitudes and they have begun to transfer their affections to this "Lamb of God" (John 1:36). It is brought to John's attention that the crowds, even some of his own disciples, are turning to Jesus, listening to His teaching and being baptized by His disciples. One gets the feeling that those who brought the news to John concerning the decline of his ratings may have hoped that they would get the chance to see John react just a bit negatively. But they didn't; he let them down.

A man can receive nothing, unless it has been given him from heaven. You yourselves bear me witness, that I said, "I am not the Christ," but "I have been sent before Him." He who has the bride is the bridegroom; but the friend of the bridegroom, who stands and hears him, rejoices greatly at the bridegroom's voice. And so this joy of mine has been made full. He must increase, but I must decrease (John 3:27–30).

CALLED PEOPLE UNDERSTAND STEWARDSHIP

Notice John's concept of life by stewardship. That is to say that his interviewers built their question on the assumption that the crowds once *belonged* to John, that he had earned them with his charisma. And if that were true, then John was losing something: his prophetic stardom.

But that was not John's perspective at all. He never owned anything, much less the crowds. John thought like a steward, and that is the quality of a called person. The task of a steward is simply to properly manage something for the owner until the owner comes to take it back. John knew that the crowd leaving him for Christ was never his in the first place. God had placed them under his care for a period of time and now had taken them back. With John that was apparently just fine.

How different this is from the driven Saul, who assumed that he owned his throne in Israel and could do anything with it that he wished. When one owns something, it has to be held onto, it has to be protected. But John did not think of things that way. So when Christ came to command the crowds, John was only too glad to give them back.

John's view of stewardship presents us with an important contemporary principle. For his crowds may be our careers, our assets, our natural and spiritual gifts, our health. Are these things owned, or merely managed in the name of the One who gave them? Driven people consider them owned; called people do not. When driven people lose those things, it is a major crisis. When called people lose them, nothing has changed. The private world remains the same, perhaps even stronger.

CALLED PEOPLE KNOW EXACTLY WHO THEY ARE

A second quality of calledness is seen in John's awareness of his own identity. You will remember, he said to them, that I've told you often who I am not: namely, the Christ. Knowing who he was not was the beginning of knowing who he was. And John had no illusions as to his personal identity. That had already been established in his inner world.

By contrast, those whose private worlds are in disarray tend to get their identities confused. They can have an increasing inability to separate role from person. What they *do* is indistinguishable from what they *are*. That is why people who have wielded great power find it very difficult to give it up, and will often fight to the death to retain it. It is why retirement is difficult for many men and women. And it helps to explain why a mother may suffer depression when her last child has left the home.

We need to ponder this matter of identity carefully, for it happens to be a very contemporary subject. John could easily have taken advantage of the crowd's gullibility during the early days when he was popular. Or he could have been seduced by their applause. The fact that the masses were switching their loyalty from the priests of Jerusalem to him could have supercharged him with arrogance and ambition. It would have been rather simple to nod yes to questions as to whether or not he was the Messiah.

You can almost hear a man of lesser integrity than John in a moment of temptation saying, "Well, I hadn't thought about it quite like you're saying it, but perhaps you're right, there is something Messiah-like about me. Why don't we just assume that I am the Christ and see what happens?"

If that had been John, he probably could have pulled off the hoax for a short while. But the genuine John would not even try. His inner sphere was too well ordered for him not to have seen through the terrible implications of a misplaced identity.

If there was a moment when the crowd's praise became thunderous, the voice of God from within John was even louder. And that voice spoke more convincingly because John had first ordered his inner world out on the desert.

Don't underestimate the significance of this principle. Today in our media-oriented world many good and talented leaders face the constant temptation to begin believing the text of their own publicity releases. And if they do, a messianic fantasy gradually infects their personalities and leadership styles. Forgetting who they are not, they begin to distort who they are. What has happened? They have become too busy to take time in the desert to get their private worlds in order. The needs of the organization become too overwhelming; the praise of followers becomes too enchanting. Thus, in the furious style of public living, God's calling voice is drowned out.

CALLED PEOPLE POSSESS AN UNWAVERING SENSE OF PURPOSE

A third look at John's remarkable response to his interviewers will reveal that the prophet from the desert also understood the purpose of his activity as forerunner to Christ. And this is another dimension of calledness. To those who questioned him regarding his feelings about the growing popularity of the Man from Nazareth, he likened his purpose to that of the best man at a wedding: "He who has the bride is the bridegroom; but the friend [that's John] of the bridegroom, who stands and hears him, rejoices greatly because of the bridegroom's voice" (John 3:29). The purpose of the best man is simply to stand with the groom, to make sure that all attention is riveted upon him. The best man would be a fool if in the middle of the wedding processional he suddenly turned to the wedding guests and began to sing a song or engage in a humorous monologue. The best man has fulfilled his purpose most admirably when he draws no attention to himself but focuses all attention upon the bride and groom.

And that is what John did. If Jesus Christ was the groom, to use John's metaphor, then the Baptizer was committed to being best man *and nothing else*. That was the purpose that flowed from his call, and he had no desire to aspire to anything beyond. Thus to see the crowd headed toward Christ was all the affirmation John needed; his purpose had been fulfilled. But only called people like this man can relax under such circumstances.

CALLED PEOPLE UNDERSTAND UNSWERVING COMMITMENT

Finally, John, as a called man, also understood the meaning of commitment. "He must increase, but I must decrease" (John 3:30), he said to those who had queried him about his attitude. No driven person could ever say what John said, because driven people have to keep gaining more and more attention, more and more power, more and more material assets. The seductions of the public life would have led to a competitive posture, but the original call to commitment from within spoke louder. What John had started out to accomplish—the introduction of Christ as the Lamb of God—had been accomplished. Having made the connection, John was satisfied and ready to withdraw.

It is these kinds of qualities—John's sense of stewardship, his awareness of his identity, his perspective about his role, and his unswerving commitment—that mark a called person. And they are the characteristics of a person who builds first in the interior or private world so that out of it will flow fountains of life.

How totally different were the lives of Saul the king and John the Baptizer. The one sought to defend a golden cage, and lost; the other was pleased with a place on the desert and a chance to serve, and won.

PEACE AND JOY

There are all sorts of special qualities in John's life worth admiring. There is a *peacefulness* about him which is not tied to the security of a career. I often spend time with men and women whose careers have suddenly been washed out for various reasons, and they become "basket cases." These circumstances reveal that their lives may have been built upon a career base rather than upon the firmness and stability of a private world where God speaks.

John reveals a kind of *joy*, which ought not to be confused with the modern-day version of happiness—a state of feelings dependent upon everything turning out all right. When others thought that John might be worried about ending up as a failure, they discovered that he actually was quite satisfied, in spite of the fact that his audiences were leaving him. Some folk in John's generation might not have thought so, but John had such an assurance because his evaluations were based first on his private world, where real values can be fully formed in concert with God.

John is in fact a called man. He illustrates what Stowe meant when she wrote that Simon Legree's blows fell only upon Uncle Tom's outer man, but not upon his heart. Something stood between John and the public evidence that he may have been a failure. It was the unquestioned reality of God's call, which John had heard in that private world of his. And that voice was louder than any other sound. It came from a quiet place of order.

BECOMING CALLED

As one looks with admiration at John the Baptizer, the obvious question is how he got that way. What was the source of this determination, this stamina, this unswerving ability to look at events in a totally different way than others did? A look at John's background will help us examine the structure and substance of his inner life.

If there is one thing that begins to explain John, it has to be the kind of parents he had, who shaped him in his earliest days. It is clear from Scripture that Zacharias and Elizabeth were godly people with extraordinary sensitivity to John's call. It had been revealed to them through various angelic visions. And they in turn from the earliest days began to pump that destiny into John's soul. We have little indication of John's family life after he was born, but we do know that his parents were marked with an extraordinary depth of integrity, godliness, and perseverance.

John's parents must have died when he was still a very young man. How he handled the loss we do not know. But when the Scripture next highlights John, he is living alone in the desert, separate from the society to which he would later speak as a prophet.

> In the fifteenth year of the reign of Tiberius Caesar, when Pontius Pilate was governor of Judea, and Herod was tetrarch of Galilee, and his brother Philip was tetrarch of the region of Ituraea and Trachonitis, and Lysanias was tetrarch of Abilene, in the high priesthood of Annas and Caiaphas, the word of God came to John, the son of Zacharias, in the wilderness. And he came into all the district around the Jordan, preaching a baptism of repentance for the forgiveness of sins (Luke 3:1-3).

These words contain a challenging insight. Caesar was in Rome doing whatever important things caesars do. Annas and Caiaphas were in the Jerusalem Temple maintaining organized religion. And various other political personalities were going and coming in public places participating in seemingly newsworthy events. Their worlds were the impressive public worlds of power, notoriety, and human connection.

But *the word of God came to John*, an insignificant man in the most insignificant of places: a desert. Why John? And why a desert?

I am reminded of Herbert Butterfield's words, which have marked me deeply:

> Both in history and in life it is a phenomenon by no means rare to meet with comparatively unlettered people who seem to have struck profound spiritual depths . . . while there are many highly educated people of whom one feels that they are performing

clever antics with their minds to cover a gaping hollowness that lies within.[2]

Why John? Basically because God called John, and he responded. The call demanded submission to God's ways, God's methods, and God's criteria for success. And John was willing to accept those terms no matter what the cost to him in pain or loneliness.

Why a desert? Perhaps because in deserts people can hear and brood upon things not easily heard or thought about in busy cities, where people are usually busy, surrounded by noise, and steeped in self-importance. Sometimes in cities the shrillness of the public life is so great that the whispering voice of God cannot be heard. And sometimes in cities, people are too proud to listen to God amidst all of their steel and concrete skyscrapers, their colorful theaters, or their incredible temples.

God drew John into the desert where He could speak to him. And when He got him there He began to stamp impressions onto John's inner world that gave the son of Zacharias a totally different perspective on his times. There in the desert he gained a new view of religion, of right and wrong, of God's purposes for history. And there he developed a special sensitivity and courage that would prepare him for his most extraordinary task: introducing his generation to the Christ. His private world was under construction—in the desert.

The word of God came to John in the desert. Such a strange place for God to speak. What can one learn in deserts? I am inclined to forsake deserts, to detour around them whenever possible. To me, deserts mean pain, isolation, and suffering. And no one cares for any of that. Deserts are hard places in which to live, physically or spiritually. But the fact is unavoidable: the greatest lessons are potentially learned in deserts if one, in the midst of struggle, listens for God's call.

In deserts, one learns about *dryness*, because deserts are dry. John would learn not only to cope with the dryness of the

---

2. Herbert Butterfield, *Christianity and History* (New York: Charles Scribner's Sons, 1949), p. 115.

desert, but it doubtless taught him to appreciate the aridity of the spirits of the people to whom he'd speak at the Jordan.

On the desert a person learns *dependence* upon God. Life in the wilderness, as the Hebrews had found out centuries before, cannot be sustained without the benevolence of a merciful God. Only a person who has suffered desert-like hardship knows what it is like to totally cast himself upon God because there is nothing else left.

There is a slightly brighter side to deserts, however. Wildernesses provide a place where one is free to think, to plan, to prepare. And then at an appointed time, like John, he comes charging out of the dry land with a message, something to say that will expose hypocrisy and superficiality. Issues are addressed that cut through to the bottomless depths of the human spirit. And an age of people is introduced to the Christ of God.

On the desert a person can be called. As John stood up first to his critics and then to the furiously defensive Herod, whose immoral life the prophet rebuked, he began to reveal that special quality of calledness. You can see it in his serenity in the midst of his prophetic performance. Something special within was operating, providing him with an independent base of judgment and wisdom. Few could withstand his message.

What was the makeup of that private world that was formed on the desert? Frankly, the biblical writers do not give us much of an answer. We are simply treated to the evidence of an ordered inner life. John is a prototype of the product we are looking for. In a public world where all seems chaotic and disordered, he moves with assurance and certitude.

Have Saul, John, and my friend the "successful bum" taught us anything? I think their message is plain. Look inside, they say. What makes you tick? Why are you doing all of that? What do you hope to gain as a result? And what would be your reaction if it was all taken away?

I look inside my private world and discover that almost every day I have to wrestle with whether I will be a Saul or a John. Living in a competitive world where achievement is almost everything, I would find it easy to join Saul, to be driven to hold on, to protect, to dominate. And I might even find myself doing those sorts of things while telling myself that I was doing God's work. But the stress of doing so can become too great.

Then there are days when I might be like John. Having listened to God's call, I can know my mission. It may demand courage and discipline, of course, but now the results are in the hands of the Caller. Whether I increase or decrease is His concern, not mine. To order my life according to the expectations of myself and others; and to value myself according to the opinions of others; these can play havoc with my inner world. But to operate on the basis of God's call is to enjoy a great deal of order within.

Sector Two

Memo to the Disorganized:

If my private world is in order, it will be because I have
made a daily determination to see time as God's gift and
worthy of careful investment.

6

Has Anyone Seen My Time? I've Misplaced It!

I had just finished a lecture to a group of pastors in which I mentioned a number of books I'd recently read. When the talk was finished, a young pastor asked, "Where have you found the time to read all of those books? When I entered the pastorate, I was sure I was going to be able to do that kind of reading too. But I haven't read anything for weeks now. I'm too busy!"

We talked for a short while about the discipline of reading, and the conversation began to branch out into other aspects of his personal life. He shared his guilt about his spiritual exercises; they were almost non-existent. He admitted that it had been a long time since he had spent anything approaching quality time with his wife. He bemoaned the fact that his sermons were usually substandard by his own evaluation. And at the conclusion of our conversation, he conceded that his failure even to read a book was merely the hint of an even bigger struggle. "Frankly," he said, "I'm totally disorganized. I'm not getting anything of consequence done."

I am very sympathetic with this young man and his admission. There was a time in my own life when I could have said the same thing. And I don't think either one of us would have found ourselves alone if our colleagues at that lecture had been honest. The world is full of disorganized people who have lost control of their time.

William Barclay, commenting upon the undisciplined life of Samuel Taylor Coleridge, writes:

> Coleridge is the supreme tragedy of indiscipline. Never did so great a mind produce so little. He left Cambridge University to join the army; he left the army because he could not rub down a horse; he returned to Oxford and left without a degree. He began a paper called *The Watchman* which lived for ten numbers and then died. It has been said of him: "he lost himself in visions of work to be done, that always remained to be done. Coleridge had every poetic gift but one—the gift of sustained and concentrated effort." In his head and in his mind he had all kinds of books, as he said, himself, "completed save for transcription. I am on the even," he says, "of sending to the press two octavo volumes." But the books were never composed outside Coleridge's mind, because he would not face the discipline of sitting down to write them out. No one ever reached any eminence, and no one having reached it ever maintained it, without discipline.[1]

Coleridge was living proof that a man or woman may be multi-talented, possess enormous intelligence and remarkable communicative gifts, and yet end up squandering it all because of an inability to seize control of time. His futile pursuits in the literary world are matched by some whose vocation is in the home, in the church, or at the office.

None of us, I am sure, wants to come to the end of his life and look back with regrets on things that could have been accomplished but were not, as happened to Coleridge. But to prevent that from happening, it is necessary to understand how we can command the time God has given to us.

SYMPTOMS OF DISORGANIZATION

The first step we may have to take is that of a ruthless self-appraisal about our habits of time use. Are we actually disorganized or not? Let us consider the traits of a disorganized life. Some of these symptoms may seem a bit ridiculous, even petty. But they are usually part of a larger picture that all fits together. Let me suggest a handful of sample symptoms.

1. William Barclay, *The Gospel of Matthew* (Philadelphia: Westminster, 1975), p. 280.

When I am slipping into disorganization, for example, I know it because *my desk takes on a cluttered appearance.* The same thing happens to the top of my bedroom dresser. In fact almost every horizontal surface in the path of my daily travel becomes littered with papers, memos to which I have not responded, and pieces of tasks that are unfinished. I can see some spouse saying, "Here, read this; he's been in your office lately." But my desk can be another's kitchen counter, work bench or basement workroom. The same principle applies.

The symptoms of disorganization tend to show themselves in *the condition of my car.* It becomes dirty inside and out. I lose track of its maintenance schedule, and I find that I am pressing deadlines for things like changing snow tires and getting the annual safety sticker.

When disorganization takes over, *I become aware of a diminution in my self-esteem.* I feel the slightest tinge of paranoia, a low-level fear that people are going to discover they are not getting their money's worth out of my labor, that they are going to come to the conclusion that I am not half the man they thought I was.

I know I'm disorganized when *there are a series of forgotten appointments, telephone messages to which I have failed to respond, and deadlines which I have begun to miss.* The day becomes filled with broken commitments and lame excuses. (I must be careful to say, incidentally, that I am not thinking of times when events beyond my control have conspired to derail even the best intentions. All of us have those kinds of days, even the most organized of us.)

If I am disorganized, *I tend to invest my energies in unproductive tasks.* I actually find myself doing small and boring things just to get something accomplished. There is a tendency toward daydreaming, an avoidance of decisions that have to be made, and procrastination. Disorganization begins to affect every part of my will to work steadily and excellently.

Disorganized people feel poor about their work. What they manage to finish they do not like. They find it very hard to accept the compliments of others. In the secrecy of their hearts they know that they have turned in a second-best job.

I have more than once driven home from Sunday morning worship services where I have preached in this sort of mood. And as I drove, I found myself pounding the steering wheel in frustration because I knew that I could have preached better if I had used my time during the week more effectively in study and preparation.

Disorganized Christians rarely enjoy intimacy with God. They certainly have intentions of pursuing that camaraderie, but it never quite gets established. No one has to tell them that time must be set aside for the purpose of Bible study and reflection, for intercession, for worship. They know all of that. They simply are not doing it. They excuse themselves, saying there is no time, but within their private worlds they know it is more a matter of organization and personal will than anything else.

If I am in a state of disorganization, *the quality of my personal relationships usually reveals it.* The days pass without a significant conversation with my son or daughter. My wife and I will be in contact, but our conversations may be shallow, devoid of self-revelation, and unaffirming. I may become irritable, resenting any attempt on her part to call to my attention things I have left undone or people I appear to have let down.

The fact of the matter is that when we are disorganized in our control of time, *we just don't like ourselves, our jobs, or much else about our worlds.* And it is difficult to break the destructive pattern that settles in.

This terrible habit-pattern of disorganization must be broken, or our private worlds will fall quickly into total disorder. We must resolve to seize control of our time.

Psychologists can suggest many reasons for people's being disorganized, and it is helpful to think some of these through. There is a large body of helpful literature available on the subject of time management and organization. But beneath the gimmicks and tricks of organization are some fundamental principles that have to be seriously considered by any person seeking an ordering of the private world. Putting these principles into practice will be a challenge for some men and women who have ignored the importance of controlling their time.

BUDGETING TIME

The central principle of all personal organization of time is simple: *time must be budgeted!*

Most of us learned this about money a long time ago. When we discovered that we rarely had enough money to do all the things we wanted to do with it, we found it prudent to sit down and think through our financial priorities.

With money, the priorities were obvious. Since my wife and I are committed to God's plan of stewardship, our first financial priority has always been our tithe and offerings. Then the fixed expenditures, food, house, utilities, books (both of us insist that books are a fixed expenditure), and so on have been set aside in amounts that we have learned to anticipate.

Only after we have budgeted these amounts of money for the necessities have we ventured into the discretionary side of the budget, namely those things that are more wants than needs. Here we may be talking about a meal out at a favorite restaurant, an appliance that makes life a bit easier, or a particularly attractive winter coat.

When men and women do not understand the difference between the fixed and the discretionary aspects of their financial lives, they usually end up in debt, which is the financial version of disorganization.

When money is limited, one budgets. And when time is in limited supply, the same principle holds. The disorganized person must have a budgeting perspective. And that means determining the difference between the fixed—what one *must* do—and the discretionary—what one would *like* to do.

These were the items I raised when my young pastor friend came to talk about why he felt so unproductive. He was surprised when I told him that we were talking about one of my own daily battles.

"Gordon," he said, "you don't convey the impression that time is ever out of your control."

I protested, "I sometimes wonder if I've ever got any of it under control." All of those symptoms of the disorganized life were at one time or another *my* symptoms, but I had made a decision (actually on more than one occasion) that I was not going to live that way for one more minute than I had to.

The Lord of Time

My young pastor friend was obviously hoping I would share with him a few of the insights that have challenged me to order my private world in the area of time use. If he thought I had a bag of answers that would make it easy, he was to be disappointed. As our conversation continued, I suggested that he take a hard look at one Person who never seems to have wasted a moment.

When I look into the Bible, I am deeply impressed with the practical lessons on organization that one can learn from the life and work of Jesus Christ. All four gospel writers present to us a picture of Jesus under constant pressure, as He was pursued by friend and enemy alike. Every word of His was monitored, every action was analyzed, every gesture was commented upon. Essentially, Jesus had no private life to speak of.

I have tried to imagine our Lord in today's world. Would He take long distance phone calls? Would He fly rather than walk? Would He be interested in direct mail campaigns? How would He handle the huge number of relationships that modern technology has made it possible for us to maintain? How would He fit into a time where a word spoken can be flashed around the world in seconds to become headlines for the next morning's paper?

Although His world was on a much smaller scale, it would appear that He lived with very much the same sort of intrusions and demands with which we are familiar. But one never gets the feeling when studying the life of Christ that He ever hurried, that He ever had to play "catch up ball," or that He was ever taken by surprise. Not only was He adept at handling His public time without an appointments secretary, He managed adequate amounts of time alone for the purpose of prayer and meditation, and for being with the few He had gathered around Him for the purpose of discipleship. Again, all this was made possible because He had brought His time under control.

It is worth taking time to ask how our Lord's command of time is demonstrated. What caused Him to be such an organized person?

The first thing that impresses me is that *He clearly understood His mission.* He had a key task to perform, and He measured His use of time against that sense of mission.

This is quite apparent during His final walk toward Jerusalem, where He would be crucified. As Jesus approached Jericho, Luke writes (chapter 18), His ears picked up the shrill voice of a blind man and He stopped, much to the consternation of both His friends and critics. They were irritated that Jesus did not appreciate that Jerusalem was still six or seven hours away, and that they would like to get there to achieve *their* purpose, the celebration of Passover.

And indeed they had a point—*if* the purpose of Christ was merely to reach Jerusalem in time for a religious celebration. But, as we soon learn, that was not Jesus' prime mission. Touching broken people like the blind man was a more significant matter, important enough for Jesus to invest His time.

Not long after the first encounter, Jesus stopped once again, this time under the branch of a tree to call down Zacchaeus, a well-known tax collector. It was the Lord's idea that the two get together for a conversation at Zacchaeus's house. Once again the crowd surrounding Jesus was incensed, first because the trip to Jerusalem was again interrupted, and second because of Zacchaeus's reputation.

From where they were standing, it appeared that Jesus was misusing His time. From where Jesus was standing, however, the time was well spent, *for it fit the criteria of His mission.*

Luke records the words of Jesus about this very fact: "The Son of Man has come to seek and save that which was lost" (Luke 19:10). The disciples had a difficult time understanding this, and Jesus had to constantly confront them with the specific facts of His mission. Until they perceived that mission, they would never understand how and with what criteria He organized His time.

A second insight into Jesus' personal organization of time is that *He understood His own limits.* When Jesus came to earth as the incarnate Son of God, He set aside certain of His rights as the Prince of Heaven and accepted, for a time, certain human limitations in order to fully identify with us. He shared our limitations but coped with them effectively—just as we must.

We dare not minimize the fact that Jesus sought time in solitude with the heavenly Father before every important decision and action during His public ministry.

There are thirty years of virtual silence before Jesus went public with His mission. Only when we are permitted audience with Christ in eternity will we fully understand the importance of those three decades. At best, we can now conclude that they were a significant time of preparation. It is impressive to realize that there were thirty years of relative obscurity and privacy in preparation for three years of important activity.

We should not be surprised, then, that Moses spent forty years in the desert before confronting Pharaoh. Paul spent an extensive amount of time in the desert listening to God before assuming apostolic duties. And the experience of these men was not exceptional.

Just before Jesus assumed public ministry, He spent forty days in the wilderness communing with the Father. Don't forget the night spent in prayer before the choosing of the twelve. There was an early morning vigil on the mountainside the day after a busy time in Capernaum. And of course there was withdrawal to the Mount of Transfiguration to prepare for the final trek to Jerusalem. Finally, there was Gethsemane.

Jesus knew His limits well. Strange as it may seem, He knew what we conveniently forget: *that time must be properly budgeted for the gathering of inner strength and resolve in order to compensate for one's weaknesses when spiritual warfare begins.* Such private moments were a fixed item on Jesus' time budget because He knew His limits. And it was very hard even for those closest to Him to fully appreciate this.

I think Jesus included a third important element in His philosophy of time budgeting, for He *set time aside for the training of the twelve.* With a world of millions to reach, Jesus budgeted the majority of His time to be with just a few simple men.

Prime time was invested in taking them through the Scriptures and sharing His heavenly insights. Key moments were spent sharing ministry with individuals and permitting them to watch every action and hear every word. Special days were set aside to explain to them the deeper meanings of His talks to the crowds. And valuable hours were seized in order to debrief them when they returned from assignments, to rebuke them when they failed, and to affirm them when they succeeded.

We might have been tempted to ask more than once why Jesus was spending so much valuable time with a group of simple-minded men when He could have taught men who could have intellectually appreciated His theological expertise. But Jesus was aware of where true importance lies, where the priorities are. And where your priorities are, there your time will be.

For reasons like these, Jesus was never to be caught short on time. Because He knew His sense of mission, because He was spiritually sharpened by moments alone with the Father, and because He knew who the men were that would perpetuate His mission long after He ascended into heaven, it was never difficult for Him to say a firm NO to invitations and demands which might have looked good or acceptable to us.

There came a time in my own life when my study of Jesus made me deeply desire this capacity. I wanted to make sound decisions about the budgeting of my time, and I wanted to be free of that frantic pitch of daily life in which one is always playing catch-up. Was it possible? Not the way I was going!

The young pastor who had come up to me at the end of my lecture remained very interested. I suggested that we get together on another day. Perhaps there would be some practical things I could share with him. But I would have to be brutally honest with him. I learned most of them the hard way.

Memo to the Disorganized:

If my private world is in order, it is because I have begun to seal the "time leaks" and allocate my productive hours in the light of my capabilities, my limits, and my priorities.

7

Recapturing My Time

The young pastor and I were to resume our conversation some days later. In the interim I began gathering thoughts about what I had learned over the past few years that had helped me begin getting my own life together in this area. What had I learned through the experience of failure, and what had I learned in talking with others in the same way that this young man was coming to talk with me?

The more I looked at the lessons learned, the more I realized how important it is to gain control of time as early in life as possible. Putting them down on paper, I discovered that there were only a few basic principles. But until those were mastered, the time issue would always be big and potentially discouraging. What I found myself writing down in preparation for my next conversation was something I came to call "MacDonald's Laws of Unseized Time." Here is what I collected.

MacDonald's Laws of Unseized Time

LAW #1: UNSEIZED TIME FLOWS TOWARD MY WEAKNESSES

Because I had not adequately defined a sense of mission in the early days of my work, and because I had not been ruthless enough with my weaknesses, I found that I normally invested inordinately large amounts of time doing things I was not good at, while the tasks I should have been able to do with excellence and effectiveness were preempted.

I know many Christian leaders who will candidly admit that they spend up to 80 percent of their time doing things at which they are second-best. For example, my strongest gift is in the areas of preaching and teaching. While I am a reasonably good administrator, that is certainly not the best arrow in my pastoral quiver.

So why did I spend almost 75 percent of my available time trying to administrate and relatively little time studying and preparing to preach good sermons when I was younger? Because unseized time will flow in the direction of one's relative weakness. Since I knew I could preach an acceptable sermon with a minimum of preparation, I was actually doing less than my best in the pulpit. That is what happens when one does not evaluate this matter and do something drastic about it.

I finally did something drastic. I had the aid of a few sensitive laymen who cared enough to help me face what was happening and show me how I might be wasting my potential. With their help I made a decision to delegate the administration of our congregation's ministry to a competent administrative pastor. It was not easy at first because I still wanted to have a word on every decision, to express an opinion on every subject. I had to back off and leave that in his hands. But it worked! And when I was able to fully trust our administrative pastor (which I found easy to do), I was able to redirect a great amount of energy into things that, God willing, I am most likely to do well.

I can almost hear someone say, "That's fine if the money is available to hire someone to fill in my weaknesses." And perhaps in some cases the only help these comments may offer is to make us realize *why* we are frustrated when time seems to escape us. But I must add that it may be more possible than we realize to find creative ways to share tasks with others. First, we must sit ourselves down and consider: who is best at doing what? This applies in the home, in the office, in the church.

LAW #2: UNSEIZED TIME COMES UNDER THE INFLUENCE
        OF DOMINANT PEOPLE IN MY WORLD

A famous "spiritual law" states that "God loves you and has
a plan for your life." Men and women who do not have control
of their time discover that the same can be said about domi-
nating people.

Because they have not set up their own time budgets, people succumbing to this law find that others enter their worlds
and force agendas and priorities upon them. As a young pastor I discovered that because my time was not fully organized,
I was at the mercy of anyone who had a notion to visit, took
me to coffee, or wanted my attendance at a committee meeting. Since my calendar was disorganized, how could I say no?
Especially when, as a young man, I was eager to please
people.

Not only was I deprived of my best time due to this lack of
organization, but my family was often cheated out of precious
hours that I should have given them. And so it continued:
strong people in my world controlled my time better than I
did because I had not taken the initiative to command the time
before they got to me.

LAW #3: UNSEIZED TIME SURRENDERS TO THE DEMANDS
        OF ALL EMERGENCIES

Charles Hummel in a small and classic booklet says it best:
we are governed by the tyranny of the urgent. Those of us
with any sort of responsibility for leadership in vocation, in
the home, or in our faith will find ourselves continually surrounded by events that cry out for immediate attention.

One recent summer, when our associate pastor and I were
both on vacation, our minister of Christian education took a
phone call from a church member who wanted me to preside
at the funeral of a distant relative of his. When told that I was
away for the month, he asked for my associate and was disappointed to discover that he was also gone. He was offered the
services of one of the other pastors on the staff, but he refused, saying, "No, I won't go any lower than number two."

His thinking was the sort that creates urgent situations for
leaders. Everyone would like the attention of the number-one
person. Every committee and board would like the number-

one person to attend their meetings, even if they do not always wish to hear his opinions. Most people in any sort of trouble would like the immediate response of the number-one leader.

One Saturday afternoon the phone rang in our home, and when I answered, the woman's voice at the other end of the line sounded quite upset. "I've got to see you right away," she said. When I learned her name, I quickly realized that I had never met this person before and that she had rarely ever visited our church.

"What is the reason that we have to visit right now?" I asked. It was an important question, one of several I've learned through experience to ask. Had this been many years ago when I was young, I would have responded immediately to her sense of emergency and arranged to meet her in ten minutes at my office, even if I had previously hoped to be with the family or involved with study.

"My marriage is breaking up," she responded.

I then asked, "When did you become aware that it was going to break up?"

She answered, "Last Tuesday."

I asked another question. "How long do you think the process of breaking up has been going on?" Her next comment was unforgettable.

"Oh, it's been coming for five years."

I managed to muffle my real reaction and said, "Since you've seen this coming for almost five years, and since you knew it was going to happen since last Tuesday, why is it important to visit with me right at this moment? I need to know that."

She answered, "Oh, I had some free time this afternoon and just thought it might be a good time to get together with you."

Law number three would usually mean that I would have given in to her desire to see me immediately. But by this point in my life, most of my time was accounted for; so I said, "I can understand why you think you have a serious problem. Now I'm going to be very candid with you. I have to preach three times tomorrow morning, and frankly my mind is preoccupied with that responsibility. Since you've been living with this situation for several years now, and since you've had several days to think about your situation, I'm going to propose that you call me on Monday morning when we can arrange a time where my mind is in much better shape. I want to be able to give you the utmost in concentration. But that's probably not possible this afternoon. How does that sound?"

She thought it was a terrific idea and could see why I would suggest that sort of plan. Both of us hung up reasonably happy. She, knowing she would eventually get to talk to me; me, because I had reserved my time for the matter that was most important on that Saturday afternoon. A seemingly urgent thing had not broken through the time budget. Not everything that cries the loudest is the most urgent thing.

In his spiritual autobiography, *While It Is Yet Day*, Elton Trueblood writes:

> A public man, though he is necessarily available at many times, must learn to hide. If he is always available, he is not worth enough when he is available. I once wrote a chapter in the Cincinnati Union Station, but that was itself a form of hiding because nobody knew who the man with the writing pad was. Consequently nobody approached me during five wonderful hours until the departure of the next train to Richmond. *We must use the time which we have because even at best there is never enough.*[1] (Italics added)

LAW #4: UNSEIZED TIME GETS INVESTED IN THINGS THAT
          GAIN PUBLIC ACCLAMATION

In other words, we are more likely to give our unbudgeted time to events that will bring the most immediate and greatest praise.

When my wife and I were first married, we found that we could attract a lot of invitations to banquets and meetings of various sorts if we were willing to sing solos and duets. It was nice to receive the warm applause and gain the popularity. But the performance of music was not our call or our priority. Preaching and pastoral care were. Unfortunately, young

1. Elton Trueblood, *While It Is Day* (New York: Harper & Row, 1974), p. 67.

preachers were not in great demand, and the temptation was to do exactly what made people want us.

We had to make a critical decision. Would we involve our time in doing what people most liked for us to do? Or would we buckle down and give our attention to what was most important: learning the ways of preaching and counseling. Fortunately, we chose to avoid the seduction of the former and embrace the latter. It paid off.

We have had to make choices like that throughout our married life. And more than once I have made the wrong choice. There was a time when it seemed successful to fly across the country to speak at a banquet. But it was a poor use of time. The old comment "A sermon is something I'd go across the country to preach but not across the street to hear" is too close to the truth to be comfortable. It once seemed glamourous to be at the head table of some politician's prayer breakfast or to be interviewed on a Christian radio program, but it may not have been a high priority use of time.

Thus, the laws of unseized time come back to haunt the disorganized person again and again, until he decides to gain the initiative before everyone and every event does it for him.

How Time Is Recaptured

In gathering material for the upcoming conversation with the young pastor, I looked back on my own experience, trying to identify the principles that, when implemented, brought some order into my private world. And when I thought hard about the process that I had come through, I found that I was able to come up with three ways of successfully laying siege on time.

I MUST KNOW MY RHYTHMS OF MAXIMUM EFFECTIVENESS

A careful study of my work habits has revealed to me an important insight. There are various tasks I accomplish best at certain times and under certain conditions.

For example, I do not study effectively for my Sunday preaching during the early days of the week. Two hours of study on Monday are relatively worthless, while one hour on Thursday or Friday is almost priceless. I simply concentrate better. On the other hand, I am at my best with people in the early days of a week when the tension of anticipated preaching has not yet grabbed my mind. I tend to diminish in effectiveness with people later in the week when I become preoccupied with Sunday's pulpit experience.

I can fine-tune that observation even further. What study time I do take is best taken early in the morning, when I have reasonable amounts of unbroken solitude. And "people time" for me is best taken in the afternoon, when I feel reflective and insightful.

Learning about my rhythms has taught me to reserve study time for the last half of the week and to plan time with people and committees as much as possible in the first part of the week. In this way, my time budget reflects and uses the rhythms of my life.

I have also taken notice of the fact that I am a morning person. I can rise early and be quite alert if I have gone to bed at a reasonable hour the night before. So it is important to me to maintain a fairly standard bedtime. We enforced that principle with our children when they were young. I don't know why it never dawned upon us that a standard bedtime as much as possible was probably a wise thing for us as adults. And when I finally saw this, I tried to go to bed at the same time each night.

After reading an article by a specialist on the subject of sleep, I began to experiment to find out how much sleep I needed. The writer suggested that one can determine his sleep requirements by setting his alarm for a certain hour and rising at that time for three mornings in a row. Then the alarm should be set ten minutes earlier for the next three days. By so continuing in three-day increments, setting the alarm back ten minutes in each period, one will finally come to a natural fatigue point, where throughout the following day he does not feel properly rested. I tried it, found I could rise much earlier than I had thought, and it added almost two full hours—valuable hours—onto my day.

So there are weekly rhythms, daily rhythms, and annual rhythms. I found that there were certain months of the year when I was apt to face abnormal emotional fatigue, times

when part of me wanted to run from people and from responsibility. I had to face up to that.

On the other hand, I saw that there were times in the year
when I had to be relatively stronger as a Christian leader because many people around me were living with too much fatigue and pressure. The months of February and March are
times like that, when all of us in New England fight the effects
of a long winter and tend toward irritability and a critical
spirit. I have learned to prepare myself to be an extra special
encouragement to others during those times. And when
spring comes and people feel revitalized, then I can enjoy my
own private time of letdown. Knowing those things were
likely to happen was a great help to me. I could plan for them.

I have learned that the summer months are a fine time for
extra reading and for spiritually preparing myself for the
coming year. But during January through March, for reasons I
have just mentioned, I plan to be with people much of the
time, because the counseling schedule is likely to jump dramatically. All of my books have been written in the summer
months; there is no way they could have been done in winter.

Knowing my rhythms, I am not surprised when I feel in-
wardly empty after a period of heavy speaking and teaching. I
cannot live day after day above the emotional line without
coming to a moment when I must dip just a bit beneath the
line of emotional normalcy to regather strength that has been
lost. Thus it is wise not to make important decisions on a Monday after a day of preaching several sermons. And if I have
pushed hard day after day during a holiday season, it is wise
for me to plan a short letdown period when it is all over.

There was once a time when I had not yet learned to take
notice of my personal rhythms. I remember coming to a particular day when everything seemed to suddenly cave in. I had
officiated at two very sad funerals in one week; I had had in-
sufficient rest for ten days. During that time I had read an
upsetting book and had not maintained my spiritual disciplines at all. My family time had been disordered for several
days, and a part of my work was at a point of frustration. So I
should not have been surprised when, on a Saturday afternoon in the midst of a small personal crisis, I suddenly began

to weep. Tears flowed that I was unable to stop for almost three hours.

Although I was nowhere near a breakdown in the classic sense, I learned from that painful experience how important it is to keep track of pressures and stresses, and how to know when and how I operate best doing certain tasks. I did not want that to happen again, and it hasn't. I was too frightened from that experience ever to allow myself to get so emotionally in debt again. My time had to be better budgeted than that.

I can now appreciate a part of a letter that William Booth, the founder of the Salvation Army, once received from his wife when he was on an extensive trip. She wrote:

> Your Tuesday's notes arrived safe, and I was rejoiced to hear of the continued prosperity of the work, though sorry you were so worn out; I fear the effect of all this excitement and exertion upon your health, and though I would not hinder your usefulness, I would caution you against an injudicious prodigality of your strength.
>
> Remember a long life of steady, consistent, holy labour will produce twice as much fruit as one shortened and destroyed by spasmodic and extravagant exertions; be careful and sparing of your strength when and where exertion is unnecessary.[2]

I MUST HAVE GOOD CRITERIA FOR CHOOSING HOW TO USE MY TIME

Years ago my father wisely shared with me that one of the great tests of human character is found in making critical choices of selection and rejection amidst all of the opportunities that lurk in life's path. "Your challenge," he told me, "will not be in separating out the good from the bad, but in grabbing the *best* out of all the possible good." He was absolutely correct. I did indeed have to learn, sometimes the hard way, that I had to say no to things I really wanted to do in order to say yes to the very best things.

Heeding that counsel has meant saying an occasional no to dinner parties and sporting events on Saturday night so that I could be fresh mentally and physically on Sunday morning. It

2. Harold Begbie, *Life of General William Booth* (New York: Macmillan, 1920), p. 178.

has meant saying no to certain speaking dates when I really wanted to say yes.

Sometimes I find such choices hard to make, simply because I like people to approve of me. When a person learns to say no to good things, he runs the risk of making enemies and gaining critics; and who needs more of those? So I find it hard to say no.

I have discovered that most people whose lives are centered on forms of leadership have the same problem. But if we are to command our time, we will have to bite the bullet and say a firm but courteous no to opportunities that are good but not the best.

Once again that demands, as it did in the ministry of our Lord, a sense of our mission. What are we called to do? What do we do best with our time? What are the necessities without which we cannot get along? Everything else has to be considered negotiable: discretionary, not necessary.

I love the words C. S. Lewis wrote in *Letters to an American Lady* about the importance of these choices:

> Don't be too easily convinced that God really wants you to do all sorts of work you needn't do. Each must do his duty "in that state of life to which God has called him." Remember that a belief in the virtues of doing for doing's sake is characteristically feminine, characteristically American, and characteristically modern: so that *three* veils may divide you from the correct view! There can be intemperance in work just as in drink. What feels like zeal may be only fidgets or even the flattering of one's self importance . . . By doing what "one's station and its duties" does not demand, one can make oneself less fit for the duties it *does* demand and so commit some injustice. Just you give Mary a little chance as well as Martha.[3]

I SEIZE TIME AND COMMAND IT WHEN I BUDGET IT FAR IN ADVANCE

This last principle is the most important; here is where the battle is won or lost.

I have learned the hard way that the principal elements of my time budget have to be in the calendar eight weeks in advance of the date. Eight weeks!

3. C. S. Lewis, *Letters to an American Lady* (Grand Rapids: Eerdmans, 1975), p. 53.

If this is August, then I am already beginning to think through October. And what goes into the calendar? Those non-negotiable aspects of my private world: my spiritual disciplines, my mental disciplines, my Sabbath rest, and of course my commitments to family and special friendships. Then a second tier of priorities will enter the calendar: the schedule of the main work to which I am committed—sermon study, writing, leadership development, and discipling.

As much as possible all of this is placed in the calendar many, many weeks in advance of the target week, because as I get closer to that week I discover that people move in to make demands upon the available time. Some of them will have legitimate demands, and it is to be hoped there will be space for them.

But others will have demands that are not appropriate. They will request an evening that I have scheduled for the family. Or they will want an hour in a morning reserved for study. How much better my private world is when I allow that work to *flow around* the priorities and into available slots than when things are the other way around.

It occurred to me one day that my most important time allocations had something in common. They never screamed out immediately when ignored. I could neglect my spiritual disciplines, for example, and God did not seem to shout loudly about it. I could make it just fine for a while. And when I did not allocate time for the family, Gail and the children were generally understanding and forgiving—often more so than certain church members who demanded instant response and attention. And when I set study aside as a priority, I could get away with it for a while. These things could be ignored for a while without adverse consequences. And that is why they were so often crowded out when I did not budget for them in advance. Other less important issues had a way of wedging them aside week after week. Tragically, if they are neglected too long, when family, rest, and spiritual disciplines are finally noticed it is often too late for adverse consequences to be avoided.

When our son, Mark, was in high school, he was a successful athlete; our teenaged daughter, Kristen, was an actress and musician. Both were in games and performances. It would have been easy to have missed those events had I not penciled the dates into the calendar weeks and weeks in advance. My secretary always kept the game schedules in the office calendar, for example, and knew full well not to expect me to commit to anything that would violate those times.

When someone would ask me to meet with him on the afternoon of a game, I was liable to take out my calendar and stroke my chin thoughtfully saying, "I'm sorry, I'm unable to do it that day; I already have a commitment. How about this as an alternative?" I rarely had a problem. The key was in planning and budgeting, weeks in advance.

What are your non-negotiables? I discover that most of us who complain that we are disorganized simply do not know the answer. As a result, the important functions that will make the supreme difference in our effectiveness miss getting into the calendar until it is too late. The consequence? Disorganization and frustration; the non-essentials crowd into the datebook before the necessities do. And that is painful over the long run.

The other day a man caught up with me and asked if we could have an early morning breakfast on a certain day. "How early?" I asked.

"You're an early riser," he said. "Why not six?"

I looked at my calendar and said, "I'm sorry, I've already got a commitment for that hour; how about seven?" He agreed on seven rather quickly but looked quite surprised that my calendar might reflect plans for that early in the morning.

I did have a commitment for six that morning. In fact it started earlier than that. It was a commitment to God. He was first on the calendar that day where He belongs every day. And it is not the sort of commitment one compromises. Not if one wants to seize time and keep it under control. It is the start of an organized day, an organized life, and an organized private world.

Sector Three

Memo to the Disorganized:

If my private world is in order, it will be because I have determined that every day will be for me a day of growth in knowledge and wisdom.

8
The Better Man Lost

The only gold medals and blue ribbons I have ever won were gained on track and cross country fields. Although I could have been a more successful runner if I had been tougher on myself, those years of competitive running in prep school and college were nevertheless an opportunity for rich learning experiences in terms of the development of self-discipline and character.

Of all those youthful experiences, the greatest lesson came at the Pennsylvania Relays in Philadelphia one spring day. On that occasion, I was the lead-off man for our prep school mile relay team, a very important position. My mission was to gain the lead in the race and, when I had completed my quarter mile leg, hand that advantage on to the second runner on our team.

For me to finish that leg out of first place would mean that our second man would receive the relay baton while back among a cluster of runners. There one risked a loss of stride in the jostling and shoving that often took place, and it could cost precious tenths of a second. That time could be quite valuable if the race was closely contested in the final lap.

Since our team had drawn the number two lane, I was curious to see who had received the "pole," or inside, lane position. It turned out to be a runner from Poly Prep with an impressive record as a sprinter in the 100-yard dash. We had competed against each other on a couple of other occasions at the shorter distance, and he had beaten me rather badly. Could he do the same when the race was 340 yards longer?

It was obvious that he thought so, because he said as much when we shook hands at the starting line. Looking squarely at me he said, "MacDonald, may the best man win; I'll be waiting for you at the finish line."

You might call it a brand of athletic psychological warfare. It partially worked, and for a moment I had to struggle to gain my equilibrium.

The gun went off, and so did the man from Poly Prep. I can remember feeling the sting of the cinders that his spikes shot backward on my shins as he seemed to instantly disappear around the first turn. Meanwhile the remaining seven runners began what looked like a competition for positions number two through eight. Before I had run fifty yards, I began to mentally prepare for finishing in second place, assuming I could make even that happen.

And that is indeed what would have happened—if the race had been shorter. Somewhere around the 300 yard marker, however, affairs abruptly changed. The man from Poly Prep, far out in front, suddenly slowed down from sprint to jog. A second later, as I charged around him now running at my peak stride, I could hear him struggling to breathe. He was barely moving. As athletes put it, he was out of gas. I don't remember in what place he finished, but I do know that I was waiting for him at the finish line, trying hard not to gloat.

I learned a valuable lesson that day at the expense of the man from Poly Prep. Inadvertently, he had taught me that even men and women of great talent and energy have to run the *complete* course before they can claim the victory. To be in front at the first turn is meaningless without the endurance to finish strongly. The race must be run at a steady pace all the way to the finish. And a good runner is even prepared to complete the course with a "kick," an extra burst of speed. Athletic talent is of little consequence unless it is matched to adequate endurance.

THE COST OF MENTAL FLABBINESS

I tell this story because it speaks to another segment of our private lives that must be consistently in the process of organization. The ordering of our private world cannot take place without strong mental endurance and the intellectual growth this endurance produces.

In our pressurized society, people who are out of shape mentally usually fall victim to ideas and systems that are destructive to the human spirit and to human relationships. They are victimized because they have not taught themselves how to think; nor have they set themselves to the life-long pursuit of the growth of the mind. Not having the facility of a strong mind, they grow dependent upon the thoughts and opinions of others. Rather than deal with ideas and issues, they reduce themselves to lives full of rules, regulations, and programs.

The 1978 mass suicide in Guyana by members of the Peoples' Temple is a poignant example of where mindlessness can lead. Allowing Jim Jones to do their thinking for them, the membership courted disaster. They emptied their minds and depended upon the functioning of his. And when Jones's mind ceased working correctly, everyone suffered the consequences. A leader had promised people guidance in the midst of a hostile and angry world. He had offered answers and sustenance. And people signed away their right to independent judgment as the price of such security.

People whose minds are not strengthened for endurance are by no means always unintelligent. They simply have never stopped to think that the use of the mind for the purpose of growth is a necessary part of a God-pleasing life-style. It is easy to fall into the trap of allowing the mind to grow flaccid, especially when there are many dominant people all around who would just as soon do our thinking for us.

Such mindlessness can be seen in an unbalanced—and ungodly—family, where one person intimidates all other family members into letting him or her do all the decision-making and opinion-forming. We have many examples of churches where lay people delegate the thinking to a highly dominant pastor. The epistle of 3 John speaks against a man named Diotrephes, a lay leader who, like Jim Jones, had virtually everyone under his control. The Christians simply surrendered thinking to him.

THE DANGER OF BEING A FAST STARTER

As in a race where the naturally talented runner springs from the starting blocks with a blinding burst of speed, there are those who enjoy fast starts in adult life—not because they are great thinkers or mental giants, but rather because of natural abilities and useful connections. They may have had the benefit of growing up in talented families, where the people around them were highly communicative and gifted in dealing with ideas and problem-solving. As a result, they may have acquired considerable self-confidence at an early age.

Such early exposures teach the young person how to lead, how to compete against others, and how to handle himself in difficult situations. The result could be called "pre-mature success." And pre-mature success is often more an obstacle than a help.

The pre-mature succeeder is usually a fast learner, able to acquire expertise with minimum effort. He is usually blessed with good health and abundant energy. He can talk his way into or out of anything, it seems. And he may conclude that he can do just about anything he sets his mind to, because things appear to come easily to him.

How long things can go on this way is anyone's guess. For a lifetime, I suppose, in certain cases. But my observation is that somewhere in his early thirties, indications of possible trouble will begin to show in the life of the naturally talented fast starter. There may be the first hints that the rest of the race in life will have to be run on endurance and discipline and not talent. And, like the runner from Poly Prep, he may start to see that the slower but better conditioned runners are beginning to catch up.

In my counseling I have met many people who are struggling through midlife for this reason. I see a startling number of exhausted, mentally empty people who have stopped growing and are spending their lives in the pursuit of little more than amusement.

I use the word *amusement* because of its literal meaning. It suggests *function without thought* (*a* meaning "without"; *muse*, "to think"). Functioning without thought leads to a feeling of personal disorganization. Who are the people who function without thought? They can easily be folk of whom it was said twenty years before, "He is going places; he can't miss." It can be the preacher who at the age of twenty-one had unusual pulpit powers, the salesman who began his career with a remarkable record of completed deals, the woman who graduated valedictorian of her class. It tends to be those who never realized that the mind must be pushed, filled, stretched, and forced in order to function. Natural talent takes such people only so far and lets them down long before the race is finished.

THE NEED TO DISCIPLINE OUR MINDS

The mind must be *trained* to think, to analyze, to innovate. People fully organized in their private worlds *work* at being thinkers. Their minds are alert and alive, taking on fresh amounts of information every day, regularly producing new discoveries and conclusions. They commit themselves to the daily exercise of the mind.

"No vital Christianity is possible unless at least three aspects of it are developed," writes Elton Trueblood. "These three are the inner life of devotion, the outer life of service, and the *intellectual life of rationality*."[1] the third aspect is the easiest for many evangelicals to ignore, thinking it too worldly and offensive to the gospel. But the dulling of the mind leads to ultimate disorganization of the private world.

I understand pre-mature success because I too discovered in my early thirties that I was coasting on natural talent and not giving adequate attention to the development of my mind. I began to see that unless I did something about it, my mind would not adequately serve me in later years when I wanted

1. Elton Trueblood, *While It Is Day* (New York: Harper & Row, 1974), pp. 97–98.

to be running at peak mental stride, doing and giving my very best.

For me it meant that if I was going to become a more effective preacher, a more sensitive understander of hurting people, and a more useful leader, I would have to take seriously the challenge of sharpening my mental capacities so that I could deal with my public world. Although I was not entirely asleep intellectually, I was not doing the hard disciplined work that would help me to be the innovative and seminal person I thought God wanted me to be.

No wonder I felt the pangs of disorganization when I faced situations where I was not smart enough to understand what was going on. Like someone with a weight too heavy to lift, I found myself more and more trying to hoist ideas and perplexities that I was not mentally strong enough to get off the ground.

Although evangelical Christians have made an outspoken commitment to Christian education, there has not always been a high enough value placed upon the development of the mind. Few of us have fully appreciated the contrast between gatherers of details and rules and skilled handlers of truth. There may be some who know a little about a lot of things, but that does not guarantee that many of us know how to think deeply and insightfully about what we know.

I have watched men and women who have pressed enormous amounts of information about the Bible into their heads. They have learned to speak a rich vocabulary of correct Christian jargon. Their prayers can be so smooth-sounding that all those about them sit in awe. We think them to be spiritual people. But at other times, we begin to see that they are rigid and inflexible, impervious to change and innovation. Their response to any serious challenge to their thought is a burst of anger or accusation.

Like others, I am convinced that Christians ought to be the strongest, broadest, most creative thinkers in the world. It was Paul who said that as Christians we are given the mind of Christ. This provides a potential intellectual breadth that the unregenerate mind does not possess. It offers an eternal, a timeless perspective in which to think. In Christ there is a foundation of truth that ought to make our ideas, our analysis of things, and our innovations among the most powerful of the age. But because there is an essential laziness and internal disorganization in many Christian lives, this is not always the case. We are forfeiting one of the great gifts God provided through Christ.

Missionary-evangelist Stanley Jones writes:

> Swami Shivananda, a famous swami in India, used to tell his disciples: "Kill the mind and then, and then only, can you meditate." The Christian position is "Thou shalt love the Lord thy God with all thy mind"—the intellectual nature; "with all thy heart"—the emotional nature; "with all thy soul"—the willing nature; and "with all thy strength"—the physical nature. The total person is to love him—mind, emotion, will, strength. But the "strength" might mean the strength of all three. Some love him with the strength of the mind and the weakness of the emotion—the intellectualist in religion; some love him with the strength of emotion and the weakness of the mind—the sentimentalist in religion; some love him with the strength of the will and the weakness of emotion—the man of iron who is not very approachable. *But loving God with the strength of the mind, the strength of the emotion, and the strength of the will—that makes the truly Christian and the truly balanced and the truly strong character.* (Italics added)[2]

For many years Admiral Hyman Rickover was the head of the United States Nuclear Navy. His admirers and his critics held strongly opposing views about the stern and demanding admiral. For many years every officer aboard a nuclear submarine was personally interviewed and approved by Rickover. Those who went through those interviews usually came out shaking in fear, anger, or total intimidation. Among them was ex-President Jimmy Carter who, years ago, applied for service under Rickover. This is his account of a Rickover interview:

> I had applied for the nuclear submarine program, and Admiral Rickover was interviewing me for the job. It was the first time I met Admiral Rickover, and we sat in a large room by ourselves for more than two hours, and he let me choose any subjects I wished

2. E. Stanley Jones, *Song of Ascents* (Nashville: Abingdon, 1968), p. 189.

to discuss. Very carefully, I chose those about which I knew most at the time—current events, seamanship, music, literature, naval tactics, electronics, gunnery—and he began to ask me a series of questions of increasing difficulty. In each instance, he soon proved that I knew relatively little about the subject I had chosen.

He always looked right into my eyes, and he never smiled. I was saturated with cold sweat.

Finally, he asked a question and I thought I could redeem myself. He said, "How did you stand in your class at the Naval Academy?" Since I had completed my sophomore year at Georgia Tech before entering Annapolis as a plebe, I had done very well, and I swelled my chest with pride and answered, "Sir, I stood fifty-ninth in a class of 820!" I sat back to wait for the congratulations—which never came. Instead, the question: "Did you do your best?" I started to say, "Yes, sir," but I remembered who this was and recalled several of the many times at the Academy when I could have learned more about our allies, our enemies, weapons, strategy, and so forth. I was just human. I finally gulped and said, "No, sir, I didn't always do my best."

He looked at me for a long time, and then turned his chair around to end the interview. He asked one final question, which I have never been able to forget—or to answer. He said, "Why not?" I sat there for a while, shaken, and then slowly left the room.[3]

That encounter became the thought-starter for Carter's book *Why Not the Best?* And it is a worthwhile story to ponder. Does not the man or woman who claims to walk with Christ owe the Creator excellence in terms of thought?

Thinking is the amazing capacity God has given the human being to discover and observe the stuff of creation, to compare and contrast each of its parts, and when possible, to use them properly so as to reflect the glory of the Creator. Thinkers see old things in new ways; they analyze hypotheses, separating out the true from the false. Thinkers sometimes describe old truths in new words and forms; they help others to see how applications to life can be made. Thinkers make bold decisions, help us see new visions, and overcome obstacles in previously unseen ways.

These are not merely the exercises of the great and the bril-

3. Norman Polmar and Thomas B. Allen, *Rickover: Controversy and Genius* (New York: Simon & Schuster, 1982), p. 267.

liant. They are the tasks of everyone with a healthy mind. As
with physical bodies, some of us may be stronger than others,
but that does not relieve us of the responsibility of using our
bodies or our minds.

It is said that even though he held over a thousand patents,
Thomas Edison felt he could only claim one invention—the
phonograph—as his original idea. All his other "inventions,"
he said, were adaptations and improvements upon ideas that
other people had left undeveloped.

It would do us good to see ourselves as sponges.
Throughout the expanse of creation God has hidden things for
humankind to discover, to enjoy, and with which to perceive
the nature of the Creator Himself. We should sponge it all up.

> It is the glory of God to conceal a matter,
> But the glory of kings is to search out a matter.
> (Proverbs 25:2)

The work of the first man and woman was to discover and
identify things God had made. Because of their disobedience
against God's laws, some of the opportunity for that kind of
marvelous work was forfeited. They now had to worry more
about surviving in a hostile world than continuing to discover
what was in it. The nature of work abruptly changed. I have a
conviction that the heavenly life will in some way recover that
original form of work.

But the principle and privilege of discovery still prevails in
part. Some discoveries come through hard physical labor,
such as digging gold out of the side of a hill. Other discoveries
are made as we observe the progress of living things in the
plant, animal, and human kingdoms. And much of the exploration of creation is done purely within the mind. We dig, as it
were, and uncover ideas and truths; then we turn around to
express them artistically, worshipfully, and inventively.

Thinking is a great work. It is best done with a mind that
has trained and is in shape just as competitive running is done
with a body that has trained and is in shape. The best kind of
thinking is accomplished when it is done in the context of rev-
erence for God's kingly reign over all creation. It is sad to see
great thinking and artistic work accomplished by men and

women who have no interest in uncovering knowledge of the Creator. They think and innovate purely for self-aggrandizement or for the development of a human system that assumes it can get along without God.

Some Christians appear to be afraid to think. They mistake the gathering of facts, doctrinal systems, and lists of rules for thinking. They are uneasy when dealing with open-ended questions. And they do not see the significance of wrestling with great ideas if they cannot always come up with easily packaged answers. The consequences are a drift toward mediocrity in personal living and mental activity and a loss of much that God meant for His children to enjoy as they walk through creation discovering His handiwork. Life under such circumstances becomes *amusement,* function without thought.

The unthinking Christian does not realize it, but he is dangerously absorbed into the culture about him. Because his mind is untrained and unfilled, it lacks the ability to produce the hard questions with which the world needs to be challenged. The challenge for the modern Christian in a secular society may be to ask prophetic questions before there is going to be an opportunity to provide Christ-oriented answers.

Sometimes, because of the massive amounts of information bombarding us regularly, the unthinking Christian longs to run in retreat, leaving heavy thinking up to a few elite Christian leaders or theologians.

Harry Blamires, in an insightful book called *The Christian Mind,* asks where there are Christians with minds sharp enough to confront a culture that steadily drifts away from God. He calls for people who think "Christianly" about great moral issues. His fear, which I share, is that we fool ourselves into thinking that we are thinking people when we are not. With a stinging rebuke against the Christian public, he writes:

> Christianity is emasculated of its intellectual relevance. It remains a vehicle of spirituality and moral guidance at the individual level perhaps; at the communal level it is little more than an expression of sentimentalized togetherness.[4]

4. Harry A. Blamires, *The Christian Mind* (Ann Arbor: Servant, 1978).

When the Christian's mind becomes dull, he can fall prey to the propaganda of a non-Christian scheme of things, led by people who have not neglected their thinking powers—and have simply out-thought us.

Just as my coach once taught me to train my body in order to finish the entire race, so I had to learn what others are having to learn: that the mind also has to be trained. The private world of the Christian will be weak, defenseless, and disorganized if serious attention has not been given to this sector of intellectual growth.

The man from Poly Prep was a better runner, but he lost. He lost because 100 yards of talent is not good enough for 440 yards of race.

When I once evaluated the order of the intellectual sector of my private world, I thankfully came to see that a few natural gifts or a few years of education were never going to make me the man God wanted to use in any part of the world where He wanted me to do work. If I was going to endure and become useful to the level of my potential, it would not be because I was talented or degreed, but because I had learned to take the muscles of my mind and work them into shape.

I had to become a thinker. I had to become conversant with the directions that history was taking. I needed to know how to grapple with the great ideas of humankind. And I had to learn how to make independent judgments about what I was seeing. It was time for me to start working—hard. Other runners were catching up, and the race was far from over. I didn't want to be a better man in the first turn and a loser at the finish line because I had talent but no endurance.

Memo to the Disorganized:

If my private world is in order, it will be because I seek to use all I learn in service to others, as Christ did.

9

The Sadness of a Book Never Read

My wife and I were browsing in an old bookstore one day looking for those special titles among secondhand books that are such a delight when found. Gail found a copy of a biography of Daniel Webster that had been published in the 1840s. It looked interesting, and since we are lovers of biographies, she purchased the book.

The cover of the book appeared worn enough to convey the notion that it had been well read. One could imagine that it had been a prized edition in the library of several generations of a New England family. Perhaps it had been loaned out on a number of occasions and brought enlightenment to a dozen different readers.

Not so! When Gail began to leaf through the old book, she discovered that the printer had failed to properly cut the pages, and many of them could not be opened until one took a blade and cut them apart. The uncut pages were clear evidence that the book had never been read! It looked on the outside as if it had been constantly used. But if it had, it was only in gracing a library shelf, or playing doorstop, or providing height to a small child so that he could sit and reach the table while he ate. The book may have been used, but it certainly had never been read.

The Christian who is not growing intellectually is like a book whose many pages remain unopened and unread. Like the book, he may be of some value, but not nearly as much as if he had chosen to sharpen and develop his mind.

PUTTING YOURSELF IN A GROWTH MODE

When a person sets out to deliberately use his mind for the purpose of growth and development as a person, new order comes into his private world. His mind—an organ largely undeveloped in many people—comes alive with new possibility when he sets himself in what I call a *growth mode.*

There are at least three objectives in developing the intellectual dimension of our private worlds. Let me offer them to you as a scheme for mental development.

OBJECTIVE ONE: THE MIND MUST BE DISCIPLINED TO THINK CHRISTIANLY

I understand this objective because I grew up in a Christian context and had the full advantage of Christian teaching from infancy.

To think Christianly means to look at our world from the perspective that it is made and owned by God, that what we do with creation will have to be accounted for, and that it is important to make choices according to the laws of God. The Bible calls this stewardship. Christian thinking looks at all issues and ideas from the standpoint of what God desires and what might give honor to Him.

A person who has not enjoyed the advantage of a lifelong Christian context is not liable to gain that total perspective easily. If he becomes a follower of Christ at a later age, it will be particularly bothersome to compare his instincts and reactions to those of more mature believers. He will tend to be hard on himself, wondering if he will ever get ahead in matters of faith.

For this kind of person, thinking will be done more by commitment than by Christian instinct. In other words, the newer Christian's reaction to a problem or opportunity is apt to be a non-Christian one, and he will then have to reverse and replace it with a learned Christian response.

The person who thinks Christianly by background probably thinks with all the proper reactions, unless he deliberately chooses to embrace a life of rebellion. But whether or not he will follow up the Christian mental response with Christian action is another matter.

I describe these two styles of thought because I have found it to be helpful to people, especially younger Christians who are struggling with the meaning of spiritual growth. They wonder why they are always just a second behind the older Christians and seem unable to catch up. The key is often in Christian acculturation, which is certainly an advantage and testifies to the importance of the Christian family. This kind of Christian acculturation is becoming less and less frequent as the world around us grows increasingly secular and drifts from a Christian base.

For the new Christian, mental growth will be in part the cultivation of the Christian perspective, the Christian response to life, and the Christian value system in the market place.

The long-term Christian has a struggle of a different sort. Although he may have an instinctive Christian reaction to most situations, his commitment may not be as enthusiastic as the newly converted believer. He simply assumes that Christianized mechanisms will work automatically. And this can be very dangerous over a period of time. Thinking Christianly without a regular renewal of our commitment to Christ leads to a deadness of religion, a boring faith, an ineffective witness to God. And we who have grown up with the gospel of Christ have to be very careful to avoid this.

OBJECTIVE TWO: THE MIND MUST BE TAUGHT TO OBSERVE AND APPRECIATE THE MESSAGES GOD HAS WRITTEN IN CREATION

"The heavens are telling of the glory of God" (Psalm 19:1). Everything God made—even human beings—has as its key purpose the reflection of the honor of God.

Unfortunately, the power of sin has tarnished the capacity of some aspects of creation to reflect that honor. In fact, sin first appears to have done its job on humanity; then, through men and women, sin systematically tarnished everything else in creation. But where man has not been able to confuse the issue, the creation continues to shout out its message: God the Creator be praised!

The growing mind, filled with the love of Christ, searches creation for these messages. Because of our spiritual and natural gifts, each of us is able to see and hear them in particular areas more than in others. And we are enabled to take this creation material and identify it, shape it, reconfigure it, or in other ways use it so that God is further glorified. The carpenter works with wood; the physician listens to the body; the musician shapes sounds; the executive manages people; the educator trains youth; the researcher analyzes, innovates, and implements with the elements of the universe.

We develop our minds for these tasks and rejoice as we do them for all that God is revealing to us out of His loving heart.

OBJECTIVE THREE: THE MIND MUST BE TRAINED TO PURSUE INFORMATION, IDEAS, AND INSIGHTS FOR THE PURPOSE OF SERVING THE PEOPLE OF MY PUBLIC WORLD

The development of the mind makes it possible for men and women to be servants to the generation in which they live. I think of the contributions of missionary-physician Paul Brand, who is credited with the development of surgical procedures that have restored the use of limbs to those suffering from Hansen's disease (leprosy). We have all been enriched by the mind of C. S. Lewis in literature or John Perkins in the area of race relations. And there are men and women whose names are not as well known: a young civil engineer who uses his expertise helping build a hydroelectric dam in Ecuador; an accountant who gives precious time to help disadvantaged people restructure themselves financially; a builder who goes into the center city and teaches men and women to rehabilitate and winterize old houses; and a computer operator who gives time to teach immigrant children to read. All of these are using their minds in ministry to others.

We do not develop our intellects merely for our own personal advancement, but we put our thinking power to work for the use of others. I remember this when I push myself in my reading and filing: I am collecting the raw material that will become a sermon of encouragement or insight for others one day. As my mind grows, it may make possible the growth of others.

ORGANIZING YOUR MIND TO MAKE IT GROW

Looking back across the early years of my life, I recall once coming to the startling realization that although I had amassed enormous amounts of information about many things, I had never really pushed myself to be an aggressive thinker. In fact, I am not sure I had ever learned to love learning.

Moving through my educational years, I had tended toward being one of those who played the margins. "Tell me what it takes to pass this course," I said, "and I'll give it to you." With rare exceptions, I adopted that philosophy throughout high school, college, and graduate school. Occasionally I would be confronted by an instructor who saw through that limited view and would push me toward a higher excellence. I never stopped to ask myself why I appreciated those instructors more than the others. It was indeed fun to be stretched, to have something better than the average pulled out of me.

But when I finally left the formal education process behind, there was no one to push or pull me, no one to require excellence except myself. And soon I learned that I would have to accept full responsibility for my own mental growth. That was when I achieved intellectual puberty. For the first time, I became serious about learning how to think and learn on my own.

How does one go about this process of intellectual organization in the private world? Let me list several ways.

WE GROW BY BECOMING LISTENERS

My intellectual organization began when I learned to listen. For someone like me who enjoys talking, listening can be difficult. But if a person is not a listener, he denies his mind a major source of information by which to grow.

Perhaps the first step in becoming a listener is to *learn to ask questions*. I have rarely met a person or been in a situation where there was not something valuable worth learning. On many occasions, I have had to generate listening by first asking questions. That has meant learning how to be a good question-asker. Right questions elicit valuable information for the purposes of growth. I like to ask men and women about their jobs, where they met their spouses, what they have been reading about, what they consider their greatest present challenges, and where they find God most alive in their lives. The answers are always useful.

In the process of becoming a listener, I have come to see that most people are eager to share something of themselves. Many older people rarely have anyone to listen to them, and they are usually wellsprings of insight. Suffering people, people under stress and tension, have much to share with those who can learn to ask the right questions. And in asking we not only learn, but we are also able to encourage and love.

We particularly need to learn to listen to older people and children. They all have stories to tell that enrich the mind and the heart. Children simplify things, often with brutal honesty. Older people bring the perspective of their long years on issues. Suffering people also help us understand what are the truly important matters of life. There is something to learn from all people if we are only willing to sit at their feet and humble ourselves enough to ask the right questions.

A second part of mental growth by listening came when I started to *visit people at their places of labor,* to see what they do, meet the people with whom they work, and so learn something of the particular challenges they face. I pushed myself to gain a new appreciation of the differing sorts of contributions people around me are making to my world. I enjoy asking men and women about their vocations: "Tell me what it takes to do a job like yours with excellence. What are the great challenges a person faces? Where do you confront ethical and moral questions? What is there about this sort of task that brings on fatigue or discouragement? Do you ever ask yourself about the ways God is present in this job?"

A third way of growing through listening comes when we *listen to mentors.* Throughout my life God has surrounded me with a chain of men and women who believed in me, cared for me, and tried to make a contribution to the bringing forth of whatever potential God placed in me. I am grateful that I was taught by my parents to listen to such people, for many of my colleagues tended to slough off the counsel and wisdom of such mentors and so lost valuable information.

Fourth, I can suggest that growth always comes when we

also *listen to our critics*. And that is not an easy thing for any of us to do. Dawson Trotman, the founder of the Navigators, had a good method for handling all criticisms directed at himself. No matter how unfair the criticism might seem to be, he would always take it into his prayer closet and in effect spread it before the Lord. Then he would say, "Lord, please show me the kernel of truth hidden in this criticism."

The truth may certainly be small on occasion, but it is always worth finding and thinking through. I have been grateful to learn of Dawson Trotman's secret. It has saved me countless bad moments when I might have otherwise been tempted to be defensive when criticized. Instead I began to learn to grow at the hands of my critics. I have seldom ever heard a criticism about myself that didn't indeed contain a kernel of useful truth. Some of the kernels have been on the small side, but they were there.

When I mentally list the most important truths on which I have based my own character and personality development, I am astonished to discover that a large majority of them came through painful situations where someone, either out of love or anger, rebuked or criticized me soundly. I carry with me the memory of a time when my missiology professor at Denver Seminary, Dr. Raymond Buker, approached me at the end of a special convocation where I had read a paper on some moral issue that was burning in the hearts of the student generation of that day. I had cut two of his classes that day to prepare the paper, and it had not gone unnoticed.

"Gordon," he said, "the paper you read tonight was a good one, but it wasn't a great one. Would you like to know why?"

I wasn't sure I really wanted to know because I anticipated a bit of humiliation coming my way, but I swallowed hard and told Dr. Buker that I would like to hear his analysis.

"The paper wasn't a great one," he said as he thumped his finger on my chest, "because you sacrificed the routine to write it."

In pain I learned one of the most important lessons I ever needed to learn. Because my time as a Christian leader is generally my own to use as I please, it would be very easy to avoid routine, unspectacular duties and give myself only to the exciting things that come along. But most of life is lived in the routine, and Buker was right: the man or woman who learns to make peace with routine responsibilities and obligations will make the greatest contributions in the long run.

But I would not have learned that lesson and grown from it, at least at that point in my life, if there had not been a man willing to rebuke me and if I had not been willing to listen and learn.

We grow through listening, aggressive listening: asking questions, watching intently what is happening around us, taking note of the good or ill consequences that befall people as a result of their choice making.

WE GROW THROUGH READING

A second way we grow is through reading. In our age of mass media, the younger generation is finding it harder and harder to acquire the discipline of reading, and that may be one of the greatest losses of our time. Nothing substitutes for what can be found when we master books.

Paul gave evidence of his own hunger for reading when he wrote to Timothy asking for parchments and books. Even at that older age, he was anxious to grow. Some of us are not naturally given to reading, and it is hard for us. But to whatever extent we can press ourselves in this direction, we should acquire the habit of reading systematically.

My wife and I are students of biography, and there is hardly a time in our home when the two of us are not making our way through two or three biographical accounts. These books have poured priceless insights into our minds.

Others will be drawn to psychology, theology, history, or good fiction. But all of us need to have at least one good book going at all times, more if possible. When I visit with pastors who are struggling with their own effectiveness, I often ask, "What are you reading lately?" It is almost predictable that if a pastor is struggling with failure in his ministry, he will be unable to name a title or an author that he has been reading in recent days. If he is not reading, the chances are strong that he is not growing. And if he is not growing, then he may rapidly slip into ineffectiveness.

During the hostage crisis in Iran, one woman seemed to stand out from the other fifty or more victims of that terrible ordeal. Katherine Koob became an inspiration to many in the embassy and here in the United States. When she returned to her home and was able to describe what kept her both sane and strong while in such conditions, she readily acknowledged that it was the reading and memorizing she had done throughout her life. In her mind was stored an almost infinite amount of material from which she drew strength and resolve as well as the truth with which to comfort others.

In my own disciplines, I have tried to set aside a minimum of an hour each day for the purpose of reading. I have found that one should never read without a pencil in hand to mark salient passages, and I have developed a simple series of codes that will remind me of impressive thoughts or quotes worth clipping and filing for future use.

As I read, I jot down key thoughts and ideas, which become the grist for sermons or articles. Not infrequently an insight jumps out that can be of value to someone I know. It has often been a form of ministry to make a copy of that particular quote or reference and send it along as a piece of encouragement or instruction.

If an author has been particularly stimulating to my mind and heart, I will attempt to acquire everything he or she has written. And I will take careful note of bibliographies, footnotes, and indexes for material worth checking into myself.

Over the years, I have learned to ask anyone I know to be a student or reader of any kind, "What are you reading?" If the person can suggest a half dozen titles, I am most grateful and put them on a reading list. You can always tell the readers in a group when someone mentions a particularly excellent book. The readers are the ones who immediately take out notebook or reference card and jot down the name and author.

WE GROW THROUGH DISCIPLINED STUDY

A third way to grow mentally is through the discipline of study. The amount of time spent studying will vary for all of us and will have a lot to do with our vocations. Preachers simply have to study if they are going to provide the sort of pulpit "feeding" that they have been mandated to do.

In my earliest years of ministry, when this business of mental growth had not yet become a discipline for me, most of my study was what I now call *defensive study*. By that I mean that I studied frantically simply because I had an upcoming sermon to preach or talk to give. And all my study was centered on the completion of that task.

But later I discovered the importance of something I now call *offensive study*. This is study that has as its objective the gathering of large clusters of information and insight out of which future sermons and talks, books, and articles may grow. In the former kind of study, one is restricted to one chosen subject. In the latter, one is exploring, turning up truth and understanding from scores of sources. Both forms of study, offensive and defensive, are necessary in my life.

We grow when we pursue the discipline of offensive study. This is done through reading, taking occasional courses that stretch our minds, taking on challenges that force us to learn new things, and exploring various disciplines for the sheer joy of learning more about God's world.

I have found that summer is an ideal time for great offensive study; winter is not. Each year I set aside certain books and projects with which I wish to acquaint myself, and when the summer months provide extra space, I get busy. It is to be hoped that by the end of the summer I will be ready to move into the heavier months of the year with considerable amounts of raw material in my notebooks for sermons and Bible studies throughout the coming year.

As I mentioned earlier in this book, my study time is best accomplished in the early morning hours. But I am able to achieve it only because I have budgeted space for it in the calendar far in advance of the date. If I cheat on the time, I almost always end up regretting it. It is a date that ought never to be broken.

I have a supportive wife who protects and encourages my study time, and that is part of her growth as well. In our early years of marriage and ministry she had to learn the importance of offensive and defensive study just as I had to. As a young wife, when she saw me reading a book or sitting at my desk, she didn't hesitate to interrupt me. After all, it was easy to surmise, what is a thirty-second interruption for a question or a quick break to take out the garbage?

But Gail came to see that study is hard work for me and that interruptions often shatter mental momentum. With that realization, she not only became a protector of my time but a creator of it, skillfully admonishing me if she caught me wasting any of it or procrastinating on my commitments. None of my books would ever have been written if she had not determined with me that my writing was the will of God and that I would need her support as well as her prodding.

Some months ago I led a seminar for pastors on the subject of preaching, and discussed the matters of study and preparation. Since a number of spouses were present when I spoke, I said to the group, "Now some of you may be tempted to think that when your husband or wife is reading, they are really expending second-class time. So you are liable to feel free to interrupt them on impulse. What you need to realize is that they are working every bit as much as the carpenter who is in his shop sharpening the blade of a saw. Within reason, you ought not only to avoid interrupting your spouses, you ought to try your best to maximize their privacy if you want them to grow in effectiveness."

A couple of months later, a couple came up to me at another meeting where I was giving some talks. They were hand in hand and both beaming. The young man extended his hand and said, "We've come to thank you for changing our lives."

Since I'm not given to thinking that I can change lives very often, I was curious to know what I had done.

The wife responded, "We were present at your seminar on preaching a few months back, and you told us about the importance of reading and studying as work. You emphasized the guarding of one another's times for that. Remember?"

Yes, I certainly remembered.

"I realized," she went on to say, "that I'd never seen my husband's reading and study from that perspective. I promised God that I would do things differently when we got home—"

"—and it's changed my life," the young pastor said. "We're grateful to you."

Studying means developing good filing systems to store my information so that it is never wasted. It means making sacrifices to acquire a good library of reference books. But most of all, it means determination and discipline. And the result is always growth.

One more comment about the importance of studying for all of us. I have talked primarily about pastors because that is my world, and because study is so important to pastors. But I am speaking in principle to all Christians, to all men and women. I have realized the importance not only of my wife's making it possible for me to study but of my making it possible for her to study. This is a mutual discipline to which we encourage one another—both of us should be engaging in growth of the mind.

I want to make clear that this means that *we who are husbands need to ask whether or not we are creating and guarding time for our wives to read and study.* In the process of marriage counseling, we talk to many couples whose problem is uneven intellectual growth. After ten or fifteen years of marital relationship, one is growing while the other is not. Frankly, we most often encounter the problem of the wife's continuing to maintain intellectual momentum into her forties while the husband prefers sitting in front of the television set. But the problem can work both ways.

You can recognize students of every age primarily because they tend to be notetakers. Many years ago Gail and I adopted a special size notebook paper and bought dozens of looseleaf binders. All of our notes go into those books under special topical codes. We go virtually nowhere without paper so that we are ready to record the thoughts of someone who might come across our path and have something significant to say. One never knows when he will turn up a book or come upon an experience worth recording for future reference.

The Christian who wants to grow will always take notes

when sermons are being preached or Bible classes are being taught. It is one practical way of asserting faith that God is going to give the listener something that will be useful in the future in the service of others. Good notetaking is one way to store the information and insights that are constantly coming at us, and therefore to take advantage of all the possible growth that is available to us.

The Old Testament scribe Ezra believed in the growth of the mind. "And Ezra set himself to study the law of the Lord, to do it, and to teach its statutes in all of Israel." The order of this description of personal growth in a man's private world is worth noting: he studied; he did what he learned; he shared what was worthwhile. Ezra was a professional student of sorts, putting in far more time than any of us will ever do. But he set a great precedent. And because his mind and spirit were full, God tapped Ezra for the gigantic task of leading a large task force of men across the wilderness to rebuild Jerusalem.

If you were to come to our home today and take that old Webster biography off the shelf, you would discover that we have slit open every page so that we could read the story of that great American's life. The book still looks terribly worn, but now it is worn for the right reason: it has finally been read!

Like the book when we found it, many people show the outer marks of the wear and tear of life. But inside large areas of their private world remain unopened. They are disorganized within because they have never stretched and conditioned their minds to handle the information and challenges of the age. They have not taken advantage of all that God has placed here for us to discover, enjoy, and use.

But when we take seriously the growth and development of our minds, a beautiful thing happens. We come to know God more fully, and we are infinitely more useful in the service of others, for in just the way that creation was originally designed, we—our sharpened minds—begin to reflect the glory of God also.

What a beautiful thing to see: a human being in God's world with a sharpened mind, having opened every page with insight and truth.

Sector Four

Memo to the Disorganized:

If my private world is in order, it will be because I regularly choose to enlarge the spiritual center of my life.

10
Order in the Garden

Howard Rutledge, a United States Air Force pilot, was shot down over North Viet Nam during the early stages of the war. He spent several miserable years in the hands of his captors before being released at the war's conclusion.

In his book *In the Presence of Mine Enemies*, he reflects upon the resources from which he drew in those arduous days when life seemed so intolerable.

> During those longer periods of enforced reflection it became so much easier to separate the important from the trivial, the worthwhile from the waste. For example, in the past, I usually worked or played hard on Sundays and had no time for church. For years Phyllis [his wife] had encouraged me to join the family at church. She never nagged or scolded—she just kept hoping. But I was too busy, too preoccupied, to spend one or two short hours a week thinking about the really important things.
>
> Now the sights and sounds and smells of death were all around me. My hunger for spiritual food soon outdid my hunger for a steak. Now I wanted to know about that part of me that will never die. Now I wanted to talk about God and Christ and the church. But in Heartbreak [the name POWs gave their prison camp] solitary confinement, there was no pastor, no Sunday-School teacher, no Bible, no hymnbook, no community of believers to guide and sustain me. *I had completely neglected the spiritual dimension of my life. It took prison to show me how empty life is without God.* (Italics added)[1]

1. Howard Rutledge and Phyllis Rutledge with Mel White and Lyla White, *In the Presence of Mine Enemies* (Old Tappan, N.Y.: Fleming Revell, 1973), p. 34.

It took the pressure of a POW camp to show Rutledge that there was a center to his private world that he had been neglecting virtually all of his life. I like to refer to this center as a person's spirit; others call it the soul. You can't physiologically locate the spiritual center of a person's private world, but it is there. It is eternal, and it is the point at which we most intimately commune with our heavenly Father. The spirit can never lose its eternal nature, but it can exist in a state of such disorganization that almost no communion with God is possible. That usually leads to a general chaos in other parts of one's private world.

The Christian is theologically convinced of the existence of the soul. But many Christians struggle with the quality of life within that center. At least that is the impression I get when I listen for very long to those who are willing to talk about the meaning of private spiritual activity. Many men and women are painfully dissatisfied with their level of contact with God. "I just don't feel like I get through to Him very often" is a typical comment.

A disorganized spirit often means lack of inner serenity. For some, what should be tranquility is in fact only numbness or emptiness. Some suffer from restlessness, a feeling that they never quite measure up to the expectations they think God has for them. A common concern is the inability to maintain spiritual momentum, to have reasonably consistent attitudes and desires. "I start out my week with great intentions," a young person comments, "but by Wednesday morning, I've lost interest. I just can't sustain a spiritual life that is satisfying. So I get to the point where I'm tired of trying."

THE QUICK FIX

A look at the great saints of Scripture sometimes makes us envious. We reflect upon the burning bush experience of Moses, Isaiah's vision in the Temple, and the confrontation Paul had on the road to Damascus.

We are tempted to say, "If I could have had an experience like any of those, I'd be spiritually fixed for life." We think our spirituality might be enhanced by some dramatic moment that would indelibly burn itself upon our consciousness. Having been so impressed by such a spectacular touch with God, we would never be tempted to doubt the matter again.

That is one reason many of us are tempted to reach out for a sort of "quick fix" that makes God seem real and more intimate. Some feel deeply enriched if they are caused to feel terribly guilty by a preacher who angrily thunders forth with accusations and denunciations. Others quest after emotional experiences that lift them out of themselves into ecstatic levels. There are those who immerse themselves in endless rounds of Bible teaching and study, making the search for pure doctrine a way of finding satisfactory intimacy with God. Still others pursue spirituality through busyness in the church. Usually our choice of these or other ways of filling the seemingly empty spirit is based upon our psychological temperament—what most effectively touches us for the moment and makes us feel at peace.

But the fact is that the average person—like you and me—is not likely to have a great biblical confrontation; nor would we be satisfied by the dramatic experiences that happen to others. If we are ever to develop a spiritual life that gives contentment, it will be because we approach spiritual living as a discipline, much as the athlete trains his body for competition.

One thing is certain. If we do not choose to take on that discipline, there will come a day—as it came for Howard Rutledge—when we will regret that we had not undertaken the challenge.

CULTIVATING THE GARDEN

How shall we describe this center, this inner spiritual territory where encounters are almost too sacred for words? Beyond the theological definitions, we are left with not much more than a collection of metaphors.

David of the Psalms was thinking in metaphors when he imagined his inner spirit to be like a pasture where God, the shepherd, led him as a lamb. In his metaphor, there were calm waters, green pastures, and tables loaded with food to be eaten in safety. This was a place, David said, where the soul was restored.

The eighteenth-century Christian poet William Cowper used the metaphor of a quiet pool:

> A life all turbulence and noise may seem
> To him that leads it wise and to be praised,
> But wisdom is a pearl with most success
> Sought in still waters.
>
> (from *The Task*, book 3)

For me the appropriate metaphor for the inner spiritual center is a garden, a place of potential peace and tranquility. This garden is a place where the Spirit of God comes to make self-disclosure, to share wisdom, to give affirmation or rebuke, to provide encouragement, and to give direction and guidance. When this garden is in proper order, it is a quiet place, and there is an absence of busyness, of defiling noise, of confusion.

The inner garden is a delicate place, and if not properly maintained it will be quickly overrun by intrusive undergrowth. God does not often walk in disordered gardens. And that is why inner gardens that are ignored are said to be empty.

That is exactly what Howard Rutledge was struggling with when the pressure was at its highest in "Heartbreak" prison. Total isolation, frequent beatings, and deteriorating health had made his world a hostile place. What resources did he have to draw upon that would sustain him? According to his own admission he'd squandered opportunities earlier in life to store up strength and resolve in his inner garden. "I was too busy, too preoccupied," he says, "to spend one or two short hours a week thinking about the really important things." Nevertheless, what little he had from his childhood, he seized and developed. Suddenly, God was a very real and very important part of his existence.

Bringing order to the spiritual dimension of our private worlds is spiritual gardening. It is the careful cultivation of spiritual ground. The gardener turns up soil, pulls out unwanted growth, plans the use of the ground, plants seeds, waters and nourishes, and enjoys the harvests that result. All of this is what many have called spiritual discipline.

I love the words of Brother Lawrence, a reflective Christian of many centuries ago who used the metaphor of a chapel:

> It is not needful always to be in church to be with God. We make a chapel of our heart, to which we can from time to time withdraw to have gentle, humble, loving communion with Him. Everyone is able to have these familiar conversations with God. Some more, some less—He knows our capabilities. *Let us make a start. Perhaps He only waits for us to make one whole-hearted resolve.* Courage! We have but a short time to live. (Italics added)[2]

Let us begin soon, Brother Lawrence coaxes us; time is short! The discipline of the spirit must begin *now.*

PRIVILEGES WE CAN LOSE

Unless we make that start, we lose out on a number of privileges that God designed in order to make us fully alive. For example, *we will never learn to enjoy the eternal and infinite perspective on reality* that we were created to have. Our powers of judgment will be substantially curtailed.

David shows us a bit of the eternal perspective when he writes of the "kings of the earth" launching movements and systems by which they think to replace God (Psalm 2:2). David would have been intimidated by these kings and movements had he not had the perspective of an eternal and sovereign God, whom he pictures as sitting in the heavens laughing over all these futile machinations. The result? David was not given to fear, as some might have been if their eternal perspective was lacking.

If the spiritual center of our private world goes undisciplined, a second privilege we will lack will be *a vital, life-giving friendship with Christ.* Again, David was very much aware of the loss of this kind of contact with his God when he sinned with Bathsheba. He could stand it just so long, and then he went racing to God with a cry of confession and a plea

2. Brother Lawrence, *The Practice of the Presence of God,* trans. E. M. Blaiklock (Nashville: Thomas Nelson, 1982).

for restoration. That intimacy simply meant too much to him.

A third privilege undisciplined spirits will lose is *the fear of accountability to God.* There will be a growing forgetfulness that all we are and have comes from His good hand, and we will fall into the rut of assuming it is all ours. This happened to Uzziah, king of Judah, who had had a great relationship with God and then let it lapse (2 Chronicles 26). The result was a growth in pride that led to an embarrassing downfall. He began a hero; he ended the fool. The difference was the growing chaos and disorder in his inner garden.

Letting the spiritual center fall into disrepair means, fourth, that we lose *the awareness of our real size in comparison to the Creator.* And conversely, we forget our *specialness and value before Him as His sons and daughters.* Forgetting these things, we make the mistakes of the Prodigal Son and end up making a series of disastrous judgments that have painful consequences.

Finally, a neglected, disordered spiritual center usually means that we have little *reserve or resolve for crisis moments* such as failure, humiliation, suffering, the death of a loved one, or loneliness. This was Rutledge's desperate situation. How unlike Paul in the Roman jail: everyone had left him, for good or bad reasons; but he was sure he was not alone. And where did such assurance come from? It came from years of spiritual discipline, of inner gardening that produced a place where he and God could meet alone regardless of the hostility of the public world about him.

WHAT WILL IT TAKE?

When the inner garden is under cultivation and God's Spirit is present, harvests are regular events. The fruits? Things like courage, hope, love, endurance, joy, and lots of peace. Unusual capacities for self-control, the ability to discern evil and to ferret out truth are also reaped. As the writer of the Proverbs put it:

> For wisdom will enter your heart,
> And knowledge will be pleasant to your soul;

Discretion will guard you,
Understanding will watch over you,
To deliver you from the way of evil,
From the man who speaks perverse things.

(Proverbs 2:10)

Richard Foster quotes a favorite author of mine, Thomas Kelly:

We feel honestly the pull of many obligations and try to fulfill them all. And we are unhappy, uneasy, strained, oppressed, and fearful we shall be shallow. . . . We have hints that there is a way of life vastly richer and deeper than all this hurried existence, a life of unhurried serenity and peace and power. If only we could slip over into that Center! . . . We have seen and known some people who have found this deep Center of living, where the fretful calls of life are integrated, where No as well as Yes can be said with confidence.[3]

Kelly says it well; if only we could slip over into that Center!

Down through the centuries the Christian mystics were the ones who took spiritual discipline most seriously. They studied it, practiced it, and occasionally carried the disciplines to unhealthy and dangerous extremes. But they believed that there had to be regular experiences of withdrawal from routines and relationships to seek God in an inner garden. They were quick to tell us that church services and religious celebrations were far from adequate. A man or a woman had to develop a chapel, still waters, or a garden in the private world, they said. There was no alternative.

Jesus certainly pursued the discipline of His spirit. We know that David did. And so did Moses, the apostles, and Paul, who wrote of his own routines:

I run in such a way, as not without aim; I box in such a way, as not beating the air; but I buffet my body and make it my slave, lest possibly, after I have preached to others, I myself should be disqualified (1 Corinthians 9:26–27).

3. Cited in Richard Foster, *Freedom of Simplicity* (New York: Harper & Row, 1981), p. 78.

Have we cheapened this spiritual discipline, this cultivation of the inner garden? Today Christians talk about the importance of "quiet time," a daily devotional often reduced to a system or method that is swift and streamlined. We boil it down to seven minutes or thirty minutes, depending on how much time we have available. We use Bible study guides, devotional guides, devotional booklets, and carefully organized prayer lists. All of which is nice—better, I suppose, than nothing—but not nearly as effective as what the mystics had in mind.

A major Christian magazine called me not long ago to ask if I would spend a day with an outstanding Christian leader from another country who was visiting our city of Boston. They wanted me to lead him through an in-depth interview about himself, so that readers could gain insight into him as a person. I called on him to request permission for the conversation.

"And what shall we talk about?" he asked me.

"I thought we'd talk about your life as a preacher, a writer, and a scholar," I said. "Perhaps we could get into your views of family life, friendships, and your spiritual disciplines—"

"My spiritual disciplines?" he broke in.

"Yes," I came back. "A lot of people would love to know something of the ways in which you've pursued a personal walk with God."

I'll never forget his response.

"That part of my life is far too private to share with anyone."

I still think that many of us who are younger men and women in ministry would have profited from this older man's insights; nevertheless, I heard what he was trying to say. This part of his private world was just that: strictly private. It had been developed in secrecy, and it would stay that way. He and God would share it together—and alone. It would not be reduced to a system.

What will it take to force us into disciplined cultivation of the inner garden of our private worlds? Will it require an experience of severe suffering? That is what history seems to say over and over again: those under pressure seek God, because there is nothing else. Those smothered in "blessings" tend to drift with the current. And that is why I question the word *blessing* sometimes. Surely something is not a blessing if it seduces us away from inward spiritual cultivation.

Can the importance of the inward center ever be appreciated until we have come close to death, defeat, or humiliation? But the command and the precedents come to us over and over again, in the Scriptures and through the history of the great saints. He who orders his inner spiritual world will make a place for God to visit and speak. And when that voice is heard, it will be unlike anything else ever spoken. That is what Howard Rutledge discovered. But it took a prisoner of war experience to force him to find it out.

Brother Lawrence says, "Let us make a start." Thomas Kelly admonishes: "Slip over into that Center!" Christ calls, "Come learn of Me." How does this discipline of the spirit happen?

Memo to the Disorganized:

If my private world is in order, it will be because I am
unafraid to be alone and quiet before Christ.

11
No Outer Props Necessary

When E. Stanley Jones, Methodist missionary to India, was an aged man, he had a debilitating stroke that left him immobile and virtually speechless. But not faithless. "I need no outer props to hold up my faith," he wrote, "for my faith holds me." But he sadly saw that his was not the experience of everyone around him.

> I was talking to a bishop who had retired. He was frustrated. When he was no longer in the limelight of the bishopric, he was frustrated and told me so. He wanted to know the secret of victorious living. I told him it was in self-surrender. *The difference was in giving up the innermost self to Jesus.* The difference was in the texture of the things that held him. When the outer strands were broken by retirement, the inner strands were not enough to hold him. Apparently he had a case of "limelight-itis" instead of a case of surrender to Jesus. *Fortunately, with me, surrender to Jesus was the primary thing, and when the outer strands were cut by this stroke, my life didn't shake.* (Italics added)[1]

Jones understood what Thomas Kelly is saying when he calls for us to slip over into the center. Who of us would not like to have Jones's perspective and endurance? But how many of us are destined, due to neglect of our inner garden, to fall

1. E. Stanley Jones, *The Divine Yes* (Nashville: Abingdon, 1975), p. 63.

into the trap the bishop set for himself? How do we cultivate the inner garden of our private worlds?

Because this book is not primarily a treatment of spiritual disciplines, I cannot survey all the ways the saints have found to strengthen the inner spirit. Instead, I have selected four spiritual exercises of fundamental importance, exercises that I find many Christians neglecting. They are: the pursuit of *solitude and silence;* regular *listening to God;* the experience of *reflection and meditation;* and *prayer as worship and intercession.*

SILENCE AND SOLITUDE

The desert fathers of centuries ago, Henri Nouwen tells us, understood the importance of a silent environment for the cultivation of the spirit when they called out to one another, *"Fuge, terche, et quisset"*—silence, solitude, and inner peace.

Few of us can fully appreciate the terrible conspiracy of noise there is about us, noise that denies us the silence and solitude we need for this cultivation of the inner garden. It would not be hard to believe that the archenemy of God has conspired to surround us at every conceivable point in our lives with the interfering noises of civilization that, when left unmuffled, usually drown out the voice of God. He who walks with God will tell you plainly, God does not ordinarily shout to make Himself heard. As Elijah discovered, God tends to whisper in the garden.

Recently I visited a missionary center in Latin America where workmen were constructing a sound studio for a radio station. They were taking careful measures to soundproof the rooms so that no noise from the city streets could mar the broadcasts and recordings that would emanate from that place. We must learn to soundproof the heart against the intruding noises of the public world in order to hear what God has to say. I love the words of Mother Teresa of Calcutta:

We need to find God, and he cannot be found in noise and restlessness. *God is the friend of silence.* See how nature—trees, flowers, grass—grow in silence; see the stars, the moon and sun, how they move in silence . . . the more we receive in silent prayer, the more we can give in our active life. *We need silence to be able to touch souls.* The essential thing is not what we say, but what God says to us and through us. All our words will be useless unless they come from within—words which do not give the light of Christ increase the darkness. (Italics added)[2]

Our worlds are filled with the noise of endless music, chatter, and busy schedules. In many homes there is a stereo in almost every room, in every car, in each office, in the elevator. Now I see that even when I dial a friend at his office I am offered music over the phone until he comes to answer my call. With the intrusion of so much noise, when can we withdraw and monitor the still, small voice of God?

We are so accustomed to noise that we grow restless without it. Worshipers in a congregation find it difficult to sit in quietness for more than a minute or two; we assume that something has gone wrong and someone has forgotten his part. Most of us would find it difficult to go even an hour without saying anything or hearing a word from someone.

The struggle can be the same in the experience of *solitude*. Not only are we often bothered by silence, but few of us are comfortable with times of aloneness. But there must be times of rhythmic withdrawal. There must be those moments when we break from routines, from other relationships, from the demands of the outer world to meet Him in the garden. It cannot be done in large meetings and spectacular celebrations.

Nouwen quotes Thomas Merton, a student of those strange mystics of the early Christian centuries who sometimes pursued solitude to an extreme. What he says about them is instructive. Why did they seek solitude?

They knew that they were helpless to do any good for others as long as they floundered about in the wreckage [of humanity]. But once they got a foothold on solid ground, things were different. Then they had not only the power but even the obligation to pull the whole world to safety after them.[3]

2. Malcolm Muggeridge, *Something Beautiful for God* (Garden City, N.Y.: Image, 1977), p. 48.
3. Henri J. M. Nouwen, *The Way of the Heart* (New York: Seabury, 1981), p. 39.

It is interesting that God's angel used silence to curb the impossibility thinking of aged Zacharias when he found that he and his wife were to become the parents of John the Baptizer. If Zacharias could not accept the word of God as it had come to him, then his tongue would be stilled for several months, and he could think about it. On the other hand, when Elizabeth, his wife, realized what was happening, she withdrew, the Scripture says, partially because that was the custom of pregnant women but also, I believe, because she needed to meditate upon the strange and mysterious things that were happening.

Then there was Mary, who, when she learned of her role in the birth of our Lord, did not blurt out all of God's plans, but chose silence. "Mary treasured up all these things, pondering them in her heart" (Luke 2:19). Christ's coming was heralded not only by singing and praise from angels but also by silence from human partners who needed solitude in order to think through and appreciate the wonder.

Wayne Oates tells us,

> Silence is not native to my world. Silence, more than likely, is a stranger to your world, too. If you and I ever have silence in our noisy hearts, we are going to have to grow it. . . . You can nurture silence in your noisy heart if you value it, cherish it, and are eager to nourish it.[4]

Silence and solitude have not come easily to me at all. I once equated them with laziness, inaction, and unproductivity. The minute I was alone, my mind exploded with a list of things I should do: phone calls to make, papers I should be filing, books unread, sermons unprepared, and people I ought to see.

The slightest noise outside my study door was a massive intrusion to concentration. It seemed as if my hearing became supersensitive, and I could overhear conversations at the other end of our house. My curiosity strained to hear what was being said. Because my study is near our laundry room, it

4. Wayne E. Oates, *Nurturing Silence in a Noisy Heart* (Garden City, N.Y.: Doubleday, 1979), p. 3.

never seemed to fail that the moment I got into spiritual activity the washing machine would decide the load inside was unbalanced, and its foghorn-like buzzer would go off, insisting that I, since everyone else was upstairs, should come and readjust the wash.

But concentrating even when there was silence became desperately difficult. I learned that I had to warm up, to accept the fact that for about fifteen minutes my mind would do everything it could to resist the solitude. So among the things I did was to start by reading or writing on the subject of my spiritual pursuits. Slowly, it seemed, my conscious mind got the message: we (my mind and I) were going to worship and meditate, and the sooner the mind got in touch with the inner garden on the matter, the better it would be.

I expect that I will fight this battle of solitude and silence for as long as I live. I want to say, however, that as time has gone by, and I have begun to reap the benefits of silent time, there has been a growing hunger for more of it. But still there is that first resistance to be overcome. When one is an activist by nature, withdrawal can be hard work. But it is a necessary labor.

For me that silence and solitude is best found in the early morning hours. So it goes in that spot on my calendar before anyone can suggest other purposes for the time. For others, it may be late in the evening. But anyone wanting to bring order to the spiritual sector of the private world must find the place and the time that fits his personal temperament.

LISTENING TO GOD

It must have been like a cold shower on an early morning for Moses when he came off the mountain after having been with God and found his Hebrew people dancing around a golden calf. For days he had lived in the presence of holiness itself, and a sense of God's glory and righteousness had been burned into his spirit. But now this spectacle! He was heartbroken.

How had it happened? While Moses had been listening to God, his brother Aaron, high priest of all the people, had been listening to the people. The input the two received was decid-

edly different. When Moses listened, he received God's revelation of the law of righteousness. When Aaron listened, he
heard complaints, wishes, and demands. Moses brought with
him uncompromised standards of heaven; Aaron caved in to
the whims of men. *It was all in the listening.*

The garden of our private worlds is cultivated not only when
we draw apart for times of silence and solitude, but also when
we begin, in that environment, to deliberately practice the
discipline of listening. I have not met many who know how to
listen to God. Busy people find it hard to learn how. Most
Christians learned at an early age how to talk to God, but they
did not learn to listen as well.

We listen every time we open the Scriptures and place ourselves at the feet of the inspired writers who unfold the mys-
teries of God. We listen, as I shall point out later on, when we
sensitize ourselves to the proddings of God's indwelling Holy
Spirit. Listening happens when the preacher or teacher of
Scripture, empowered by God's Spirit, brings instruction.

All these things are worth discussing (not to mention
doing!). But right now I would like to talk about another exercise, one that can form a base for all the other ways of listening.

JOURNAL KEEPING—A WAY TO LISTEN TO GOD

When I studied some of the mystic and contemplative
Christians, I found that one practical way to learn to listen to
God speak in the garden of my private world was to keep a
journal. With a pencil in hand ready to write, I found that
there was an expectancy, a readiness to hear anything God
might wish to whisper through my reading and reflection.

That discovery came almost twenty years ago, while I was
reading a biography. The subject of the book had maintained a
lifelong habit of recording his spiritual pilgrimage. I was now
benefitting from that discipline, even though he had been
writing more for his own benefit than for mine. As he had
been tutored by God's Spirit, he had kept careful notes. What
a tool that must have been—something to go back to again
and again and trace the hand of God upon his life.

I became impressed by the fact that many, many godly men

and women down through the centuries had also kept journals, and I began to wonder if they had not put their fingers upon an aid to spiritual growth. To satisfy my curiosity, I decided to experiment and began keeping one for myself.

At first it was difficult. I felt self-conscious. I was worried that I would lose the journal or that someone might peek inside to see what I'd said. But slowly the self-consciousness began to fade, and I found myself sharing in the journal more and more of the thoughts that flooded my inner spirit. Into the journal went words describing my feelings, my fear and sense of weakness, my hopes, and my discoveries about where Christ was leading me. When I felt empty or defeated, I talked about that too in the journal.

Slowly I began to realize that the journal was helping me come to grips with an enormous part of my inner person that I had never been fully honest about. No longer could fears and struggles remain inside without definition. They were surfaced and confronted. And I became aware, little by little, that God's Holy Spirit was directing many of the thoughts and insights as I wrote. On paper, the Lord and I were carrying on a personal communion. He was helping me, in the words of David, to "search my heart." He was prodding me to put words to my fears, shapes to my doubts. And when I was candid about it, then there would often come out of Scripture or from the meditations of my own heart, the reassurances, the rebukes, and the admonishments that I so badly needed. But this began to happen only when the journal was employed.

Because I found that my prayers often seemed disconnected and that I was not able to concentrate (or even stay awake), I often wondered if I could ever develop a vigorous worship and intercessory life. Again, the journal provided a vehicle for writing prayers when my spoken prayers lacked cohesiveness. Now prayer content became sensible, and I began to enjoy recording my progress as a believer and a follower of Christ.

A key contribution of the journal became its record of not only the good moments, but the bad times as well. When there came times of discouragement, even of despair, I was able to describe my feelings and tell how God's Spirit ultimately ministered to me to strengthen my resolve. These became special passages to look back upon; they helped me celebrate the power of God in the midst of my own weakness.

I am reminded that the Lord once had the Israelites save "three quarts of manna" (Exodus 16:33, TLB) so that they would have a tangible reminder of His constant care. The journal became my "three quarts," for in it I had all the testimony I needed to the faithfulness of God in my life. This remembering process, which a journal provides, is very significant.

Today after twenty years of journal keeping, I have acquired a habit. Hardly a morning passes that I do not open the journal and record the things I hear God saying through my reading, meditation, and daily experience. When the journal opens, so does the ear of my heart. If God is going to speak, I am ready to listen.

When W. E. Sangster was a young pastor in England, he grew increasingly restive about the spiritual climate in the English Methodist church. Brooding upon his own role in future leadership, he turned to his journal to sharpen his thinking. In it he could lay out his innermost thoughts and meditations on paper and perceive what God was laying on his heart. Reading his thoughts several decades later reveals how one man used a journal to bring order to his private world so that he could later be used to press order into his outer world. One day he wrote:

> I feel a commission to work under God for the revival of this branch of His Church—careless of my own reputation; indifferent to the comments of older and jealous men. I am thirty-six. If I am to serve God in this way, I must no longer shrink from the task— but do it.

> I have examined my heart for ambition. I am certain it is not there. I hate the criticism I shall evoke and the painful chatter of people. Obscurity, quiet browsing among books, and the service of simple people is my taste—but by the will of God, this is my task. . . .

> Bewildered and unbelieving, I heard the voice of God saying to me, "I want to sound the note through you." O God, did ever an

apostle shrink from his task more? I dare not say "No" but, like Jonah, I would fain run away.

God help me. God help me. What is the initial task? To call Methodism back to its real work.[5]

Sangster's words offer a beautiful example of a man listening to God in his private world through the use of a journal. He put his dreams on paper in order to separate destructive ambition from genuine call. He searched for hints that his thoughts were not those of his heavenly Father. He wrestled with self-doubt. Isn't it interesting that, as he perceived the divine whisper, he transformed into print the still, small voice of his Lord?

HOW TO JOURNAL

When I have spoken in public on "journaling," I have found that many people are intensely interested and have many questions. Their initial curiosity tends to center on technique more than anything else. What does your journal look like? How often do you write in it? What sort of things do you include? Isn't it really just a diary? Do you let your wife read your journal? Although I am by no means an expert journal keeper, I endeavor to answer as best I can.

My own journals are spiral bound notebooks, which I purchase at an office supply store. They are rather unimpressive in appearance. I can complete one of these notebooks in about three months. The virtue of their smaller size lies not only in portability but in the fact that, should one ever be lost, I would not have misplaced a year or more of writing.

I write in my journal almost every day, but I am not overly disturbed if an occasional day passes without an entry. I have made it a habit to write in the earliest moments of my time of spiritual exercise, and for me that means the first thing in the morning.

And what is in there? An account of things that I accomplished in the preceding day, people I met, things I learned, feelings I experienced, and impressions I believe God wanted me to have.

5. Paul Sangster, *Doctor Sangster* (New York: Epworth, 1962), p. 109.

As I said before, I include prayers if I feel like writing them down, insights that come from reading the Bible and other spiritual literature, and concerns I have about my own personal behavior. I love to record things I am seeing in the lives of members of my family. I anticipate that someday our children will read through some of these journals, and if I can posthumously affirm them for things I see in their growing lives today, it will be a treasure for them.

All of this is part of listening to God. As I write, I am aware that what I am writing may actually be what God wants to tell me. I dare to presume that His Spirit is often operative in the things I am choosing to think about and record. And it becomes important to search my heart to see what conclusions He may be engendering, what matters He wishes to remind me about, what themes He hopes to stamp upon my private world.

On one recent occasion, as I was contemplating an enormous challenge I was facing in my ministry, my journal caught these reflective words:

Lord, what do I really know about drawing upon your strength? I, with the shallow mind, the weak spirit, the minimal discipline. What is there of me that you could use? I have talents, but others have more and use them better. I have experience, but others have greater and have profited deeper. So what is there?

Perhaps the answer lies somewhere in [Hudson] Taylor's comment: "God uses men who are weak and feeble enough to lean on him." But, Lord, I worry that while I may be weak enough, will I be smart enough to know from whence comes my help?

Should you ordain that I do this task, what will sustain me? What of the sleepless nights when I shall be so lonely? The seductions toward applause? The temptation to believe the symbols of leadership? What will keep my judgments clear, my mind sharp, my spirit filled? Now I ask honestly, am I able to receive this cup? What will convince me of the needs of the lost? What will keep me sensitive to the poor? What will make me listen? Pray? Study? Remain simple? O God, nothing but a visitation from Thee.

As I write on consecutive pages of the journal, I also write from the back page toward the front. The back pages hold my list of people and concerns that I have chosen to make a matter of intercessory prayer. At the top of those pages I've written the phrase "Does my prayer list reflect the people and programs to which I am most committed?"

Then, continuing to work from the back pages toward the center of the journal, I often put in excerpts from my current reading that particularly impress me. Often, I will take time to simply read through many of these brief paragraphs. They may be prayers, reflective comments from the writings of people like St. Thomas, A. W. Tozer, and Amy Carmichael, or portions of Scripture.

When the daily record beginning at the front of the journal meets the daily reflections coming from the rear, I simply close the volume out and begin a new one. It has become one more scrapbook portraying my spiritual journey, with its struggles and its learning experiences. And the pile of spiritual scrapbooks continues to grow. Should our house ever begin to burn, and assuming all the family is properly evacuated, I think these journals would be the first things I would try to grab and take out the door with me.

Does my wife read my journals? I suppose she has occasionally sneaked a look. But frankly my handwriting is poor, and I do employ a sort of shorthand; so I suspect that she would have her hands full trying to decipher anything that I might have said. Our relationship is quite intimate enough, however, that there is little in there that would surprise her.

To those who are concerned about a potential lack of privacy in such matters, I suggest that they simply find a place where the journal could be locked up and kept from those you would rather not have see inside. If confidentiality is important, you should be able to find a way to maintain it. Worry about privacy is not an adequate reason for not attempting a journal.

Journal keeping becomes a habit for most people if they will stick with it for the better part of a year. Most people quit too quickly, never achieving the habit pattern, and that is unfortunate.

My journal accompanies me on trips. It helps me to maintain a record of those I have met, so that when I return again to places where I have visited, I can simply review my previous visit in the journal and pick up relationships where they may have been suspended due to distance.

This discussion of journal keeping has led me to talk of its benefits as regards interpersonal relationships. These benefits are certainly great. But the main value of a journal is as a tool for listening to the quiet Voice that comes out of the garden of the private world. Journal keeping serves as a wonderful tool for withdrawing and communing with the Father. When I write, it is as if I am in direct conversation with Him. And there is that sense that in the words that you are led to write, God's Spirit is mysteriously active, and communion at the deepest level is happening.

My mind goes back to Howard Rutledge in his prison camp. Every voice was a hostile one; every noise introduced the possibility of something about to go wrong. In such an ugly place, was there a friendly voice, a lovely sound to be heard anywhere? Yes, if you have trained your ears to hear in the inner garden. There the greatest of all sounds may be heard: those belonging to Him who seeks our companionship and growth. In the words of an old and very sentimental hymn:

> He speaks, and the sound of his voice
> Is so sweet the birds hush their singing.
>   (C. Austin Miles, "In the Garden")

Memo to the Disorganized:

If my private world is in order, it will be because I absorb the words of Christ into my attitudes and actions.

12
Everything Has to Be Entered

E. Stanley Jones was not always the sort of person who could say, on a painful deathbed, "The innermost strands are the strongest. I need no outer props to hold up my faith, for my faith holds me." In the early days of his ministry there had come a temporary sinkhole collapse. For more than a year he had languished in both spiritual and physical ineffectiveness. "The spiritual sag brought on a physical sag," he wrote. "The outer collapse took place because the inner experience could not sustain it. I had made it a life motto that I would not preach what I was not experiencing, so the outer and the inner came together in collapse."[1]

The discipline of the spirit—what I have called the cultivation of the inner garden—depends upon the willingness of men and women of Christ to seek solitude and silence and to listen for the whisper of God.

But the things that we hear in solitude and silence must be internalized. I am writing this book with the technical assistance of a computer and a word processing program. When I first became acquainted with my computer, I had to learn the function of the "enter" key. The teaching manual instructed me that I could type anything I wanted on the screen in front of me. But until I touched the "enter" key, the com-

1. E. Stanley Jones, *Song of Ascents* (Nashville: Abingdon, 1968), p. 104.

puter would not "hear" or respond to a single word I had typed. All of my words, no matter how impressive, would just sit on the screen's surface until I entered them onto the heart (the "memory") of the computer.

I also have the ability to hear things *but not necessarily enter them.* What sits in my mind does not necessarily penetrate my heart.

Salvation Army evangelist Commissioner Samuel Logan Brengle, speaking of his spiritual disciplines, wrote:

> I do a lot of listening. Prayer, you know, is not meant to be a monologue, but a dialogue. It is a communion, a friendly talk. While the Lord communicates with me mainly through His Word, he gives me a great deal of comfort in a direct manner. By "comfort" I do not mean cuddling or coddling, but *assurance*—assurance of His presence with me and His pleasure in my service. It is like the comfort given by a military commander to his soldier or envoy whom he sends on a difficult mission: "You go, put on your armor, I'm watching you, and I'll send you all the reinforcements you need as they are needed." I have to be comforted that way a great deal. I don't just assume that God is near me and pleased with me; I must have a fresh witness daily.[2]

The Bible tells of another Samuel, a young boy interning in the Tabernacle under the discipleship of Eli, the high priest. In the night Samuel heard a voice calling his name. Running to Eli's bed, he assumed that he was being summoned for some task. But Eli had not called, and Samuel returned to his room. But the call came again and again. It was Eli who put things together and suggested how Samuel could respond the next time. "When you hear the voice again, Samuel, respond with these words: 'Speak, Lord, for your servant hears! In others words, Samuel, push the "enter" key.

Samuel did, and God spoke. The words of God penetrated his heart and changed his destiny.

We strengthen the innermost strands, as Jones put it, by making sure that God's words are entering the garden of our private worlds. Our first step in spiritual discipline is finding solitude and silence; the second step is learning to listen to

2. Clarence W. Hall, *Samuel Logan Brengle: Portrait of a Prophet* (Chicago: Salvation Army Supply & Purchasing Dept., 1933), p. 185.

God. The third step, the pushing of the "enter" key, is done through *reflection and meditation.*

Some Christians are uneasy and negative about the mention of such words. They think such practices can open a door to activity that is too undirected and that can lead to misguided conclusions. They conjure up images of people sitting in lotus positions and engaging in trancelike activities.

But the Bible is full of reflective or meditative passages and calls us to open our private worlds to them. Among the most popular are those passages out of the Psalms where the writer fixes his mind upon certain aspects of God's being and consistent care for His children.

The psalmist looked through all sorts of meditative lenses. For example, he saw God as a shepherd, as a commanding general, as a director of spiritual exercise.

The act of meditation is like tuning the spirit to heavenly frequencies. One takes a portion of Scripture and simply allows it to enter into the deepest recesses of self. There are often several different results: cleansing, reassurance, the desire to praise and give thanksgiving. Sometimes meditation on something of God's nature or His actions opens the mind to new guidance or a new awareness of something the Lord may be trying to say to us.

In his book of prayers John Baillie reveals a meditational mood when he prays:

> Almighty God, in this quiet hour I seek communion with thee. From the fret and fever of the day's business, from the world's discordant noises, from the praise and blame of men, from the confused thoughts and vain imaginations of my own heart, I would now turn aside and seek the quietness of thy presence. All day long have I toiled and striven; but now in the stillness of heart and the clear light of thine eternity, I would ponder the pattern my life is weaving.[3]

Meditation of course can be done only when we have chosen an environment where there will be adequate amounts of time, silence, and privacy. One does not get much meditation

3. John Baillie, *A Diary of Private Prayer* (New York: Charles Scribner's Sons, 1949), p. 27.

done on a bus or when driving in traffic—although I have heard people claim that was their time for the spiritual discipline.

Many of us will discover that it takes preparatory time in order to meditate. You may have had the experience of coming in from heavy exercise still breathing very hard. You know that it is virtually impossible to sit down for several minutes and be still. There is too much gasping and the catching of breath for quiet sitting. The same is true in reflection. We often enter the chamber to meet with God while we are still emotionally out of breath. It is hard at first to concentrate our thoughts and to bring them into the presence of the Lord. We have to quietly relax for a short season while the mind accustoms itself to spiritual activity in the "garden" environment. Thus, it will take time—time some people are reluctant to give.

Christians have always considered the Bible to be the central revelation of our faith and worthy of meditation. Let me add that reading the great classics of Christian literature is a must for spiritual growth. Down through the centuries there have been men and women who have recorded their insights and exercises for us to read. And although these books do not carry the authoritative power of the Bible itself, they nevertheless contain an enormous amount of spiritual food.

Reflection and meditation demand a certain amount of imagination. We read the first psalm, for example, and picture a tree planted by a river. What is true about that tremendous tree to which the writer likens the man or woman who walks after God? In Psalm 19 we let our minds sweep across the universe and imagine the celestial bodies and their incredible message. When we read the passages describing Jesus' ministry, our reflecting minds place ourselves right into the story: we see the Savior heal, hear Him teach, and respond to His directives. In meditation we latch onto phrases from the prophets, perhaps memorizing small portions, and we allow the words to trickle down over the structures of our inner being as we repeat them over and over again. From such exercises come new and wonderful conclusions. The word of God is *entering* our private worlds. And because we have fixed our attention upon His word, we can be sure the Holy Spirit will guide our meditations.

C. S. Lewis, writing to an American friend, speaks of reflective exercises:

> We all go through periods of dryness in our prayers, don't we? I doubt . . . whether they are necessarily a bad symptom. I sometimes suspect that what we *feel* to be our best prayers are really our worst; that what we are enjoying is the satisfaction of apparent success, as in executing a dance or reciting a poem. Do our prayers sometimes go wrong because we insist on trying to talk to God when He wants to talk with us. Joy tells me that once, years ago, she was haunted one morning by a feeling that God wanted something of her, a persistent pressure like the nag of a neglected duty. And till mid-morning she kept on wondering what it was. But the moment she stopped worrying, the answer came through as plain as a spoken voice. It was "I don't want you to *do* anything. I want to *give* you something"; and immediately her heart was peace and delight. St. Augustine says, "God gives where He finds empty hands." A man whose hands are full of parcels can't receive a gift. Perhaps these parcels are not always sins or earthly cares, but sometimes our own fussy attempts to worship Him in *our* way. Incidentally, what most often interrupts my own prayers is not great distractions but tiny ones—things one will have to do or avoid in the course of the next hour.[4]

Here is a good example of the exercise of reflection and meditation. God speaks; we listen, and the message is entered within the heart. The need for outer props is lessened; the inner garden is further cultivated. The man or woman of spiritual discipline is growing strong in the private world.

4. C. S. Lewis, *Letters to an American Lady* (Grand Rapids: Eerdmans, 1975), p. 73.

Memo to the Disorganized:

If my private world is in order, it will be because I have begun to pursue the discipline of seeing events and people through the eyes of Christ so that my prayers reflect my desire to be in alignment with His purposes and promises for them.

13
Seeing Through Heaven's Eyes

In an insightful little book on contemplative faith written more than sixty years ago, a European Christian by the name of Bridget Herman wrote:

> When we read the lives of the saints, we are struck by a certain large leisure which went hand in hand with a remarkable effectiveness. They were never hurried; they did comparatively few things, and these not necessarily striking or important; and they troubled very little about their influence. Yet they always seemed to hit the mark; every bit of their life told; their simplest actions had a distinction, an exquisiteness which suggested the artist. The reason is not far to seek. Their sainthood lay in their habit of referring the smallest actions to God. They lived in God; they acted from a pure motive of love towards God. They were as free from self-regard as from slavery to the good opinion of others. God saw and God rewarded: what else needed they? They possessed God and possessed themselves in God. Hence the inalienable dignity of these meek, quiet figures that seem to produce such marvelous effects with such humble materials.[1]

The fourth way we can enhance communion with God in the garden of our private worlds is through *prayer as worship and intercession.* This is what Bridget Herman says characterized

---

1. E. Herman, *Creative Prayer* (Cincinnati: Forward Movement, n.d.), p. 16.

the saints. "Their sainthood lay in their habit of referring the smallest actions to God."

"Let inward prayer be your last act before you fall asleep and the first act when you awake," Thomas Kelly wrote. "And in time you will find as did Brother Lawrence, that 'those who have the gale of the Holy Spirit go forward even in sleep.'"[2]

Most of us have never experienced this. Daily, disciplined prayer is one of the most difficult exercises Christians undertake.

Married men will often admit, for example, that praying with their wives is a very difficult thing. Why? They really don't have an answer. Sometimes pastors in a moment of self-revelation will reveal that the integrity of their prayer life is usually an embarrassment to them. And they also are hard pressed to explain it.

My impression after visiting with many Christians is that worship and intercession rank at the top of any list of spiritual struggles. No one would deny that prayer is important; but few believe their prayer life to be adequately developing. And this is a major reason the inner gardens of so many private worlds are in a state of disorder. It is why most of us would have a hard time saying, like E. Stanley Jones, "No outer props are necessary."

WHY WE HAVE TROUBLE PRAYING

Why do so many people have struggles when it comes to prayer? Let me suggest three possible reasons.

WORSHIP AND INTERCESSION SEEM TO BE UNNATURAL ACTS

Men and women were originally created to desire communion with God. But the effects of sin have dulled most of that original human desire. Sin turned a natural activity into an unnatural function.

My suspicion is that when sin affected man so deeply, it touched his spiritual dimensions most severely of all, while leaving the original physical appetites and desires virtually

2. Thomas R. Kelly, *A Testament of Devotion* (New York: Harper & Row, 1941), p. 39.

undiminished. Our instinctive preoccupations with food, sexual pleasure, and security are probably close to their original levels. It may be helpful to speculate that man in his sinless nature once probably had as great, if not greater, desire for communion with the Creator as he has for the satisfaction of the natural and very real appetites and instincts that we live with today. But the spiritual hunger, once undoubtedly powerful, has been terribly dulled by the power of sin. Thus, worship and intercession have become difficult challenges.

As a result, praying in any meaningful way militates against virtually everything within our natural selves and is foreign to what our culture teaches us as a way of life.

And that is the heart of the trouble. Few people realize how brainwashed each of us is. Messages bombard our private worlds everyday, telling us that anything of a spiritual nature is really a waste of time. From our earliest years we are subtly taught that the only way to achieve anything is through action. But prayer seems to be a form of inaction. To the person with a disordered private world, it does not seem to accomplish anything.

Until we believe that prayer is indeed a real and highly significant activity, that it does in fact reach beyond space and time to the God who is actually there, we will never acquire the habits of worship and intercession. In order to gain these habits, we must make a conscious effort to overcome the part of us that thinks that praying is not a natural part of life.

WORSHIP AND INTERCESSION ARE TACIT ADMISSIONS OF WEAKNESS

A second reason people find it difficult to enter into worship and intercession is that these acts are by nature admissions of personal weakness. In the acts of prayer, something within the inner garden acknowledges that we are utterly dependent upon the One to whom we address our words.

Now we can *say* that we are weak people, and we can *say* that we depend upon God for all of our sustenance; but the fact is that something deep within us is not willing to *recognize* it. There is something deep within that vigorously denies our dependence.

I have often been fascinated with the reluctance of many

Christian men to pray with their wives, or to feel free to take prayer leadership in a mixed group. It is not unusual for a Christian wife to complain, "My husband never prays with me, and I can't understand it."

The answer may lie in the fact that men have been taught in our culture never to reveal weakness or to engage in any activity that may show it. Prayer in its most authentic form acknowledges that we are weak and dependent upon our God. Something in the male knows this and unconsciously fights having to identify with the fact of dependence.

On the other hand, it is my observation that most women, at least until recently, have never had to struggle to face their own weaknesses; and that may be one reason that, as a group, they feel more at ease in prayer than men.

A person shows significant spiritual growth when he finds it possible to admit that he needs a relationship with God in order to be the human being he was created to be. There is an enormous sense of liberation in that realization.

Brother Lawrence wrote:

> We must examine with care what are the virtues of which we stand most in need, what are those which are most difficult to win, the sins to which we most often fall, and the most frequent and inevitable occasions of our falling. We must turn to God in complete confidence in the hour of battle, abide strongly in the presence of his divine majesty, worship him humbly, and set before him our woes and our weaknesses. And thus we shall find in him all virtues though we may lack them all.[3]

Brother Lawrence seemed never to have any problems facing up to his weaknesses, and that is one reason his prayer life was so alive.

PRAYER SOMETIMES SEEMS TO BE UNRELATED TO ACTUAL RESULT

A third reason prayer comes hard to us is the fact that it seems frequently unrelated to actual results. Lest you think I am guilty of denying a substantial teaching of Scripture, hear me carefully. I do in fact believe that God answers prayer. But

3. Brother Lawrence, *The Practice of the Presence of God*, trans. E. M. Blaiklock (Nashville: Thomas Nelson, 1982), p. 70.

most of us have had enough experience to realize that His answers do not always come in forms or on schedules that we would have designed.

As a very young pastor, I used to confess my confusion about this matter of personal prayer to my wife. "Sometimes it seems as if, on those weeks when I pray very little, my sermons come out very powerful. And on those weeks when I feel that I've really done my prayer work, I seem to preach my worst. Now you tell me," I'd challenge her, "what does God expect me to do when He doesn't seem to give me, pound for pound, the blessings that match my prayer investment?"

Like others, I have prayed for healings, for miracles, for guidance, and for assistance. Frankly, there were times I was sure God would answer me because I had mustered strong feelings of faith. But many of those times nothing happened—or if it did, it was entirely unlike what I had anticipated.

We live in a society that is reasonably organized. Put a letter in the box, and it usually ends up where you want it to go. Order an item from a catalog, and it usually comes to you in the right size, color, and model. Ask someone to provide you a service, and it is reasonable to expect that it will work out that way. In other words, we are used to results in response to our arrangements. That is why prayer can be discouraging for some of us. How can we predict the result? We are tempted to abandon prayer as a viable exercise and to try getting the results ourselves.

But the fact is that my prayer life cannot be directly tied to the results I expect or demand. I have had many opportunities by now to see that the things I want God to do in response to my prayers can be unhealthy for me. I have begun to see that *worship and intercession are far more the business of aligning myself with God's purposes than asking Him to align with mine.*

Henri Nouwen says it best when he writes:

Prayer is a radical conversion of all our mental processes because in prayer we move away from ourselves, our worries, preoccupation, and self-gratification—and direct all that we recognize as ours to God in the simple trust that through his love all will be made new.[4]

When our Lord came to the garden on the night of His crucifixion, His prayer just before His capture centered on affirming His oneness with the Father's purposes. This is mature praying.

Many times I have gone to prayer with results in mind. I wanted to gain control over the people and events I was praying about by dictating to the Father my views on how things should come out. When I do this, I am looking at people and events through an earthly lens and not a heavenly one. I am praying as though I know better than God what is best for the outcome.

Thomas Kelly suggests that a more proper kind of prayer is, "Lord, be thou my will." Perhaps among the purest prayers we can pray is simply to ask, "Father, may I see earth through heaven's eyes."

Again Kelly writes:

> The life that intends to be wholly obedient, wholly submissive, wholly listening, is astonishing in its completeness. Its joys are ravishing, its peace profound, its humility the deepest, its power world shaking, its love enveloping, its simplicity that of a trusting child.[5]

It was this kind of thinking that helped me overcome the obstacles to worship and intercession that have often been quite real to me. Yes, praying is unnatural for the natural man. But Christ has entered life, and what once was unnatural now becomes natural if I ask for the power to make it so. Yes, praying signals weakness and dependence. But that is the truth about me, and I am healthier for coming to grips with it. And yes, the answers to my prayers do not always coincide with my expectations. But the problem is in my expectations—not in the capacities or sensitivities of God.

---

4. Henri J. M. Nouwen, *Clowning in Rome* (Garden City, N.Y.: Image, 1979), p. 73.
5. Kelly, p. 54.

Having encountered these obstacles, how do we develop the discipline of worship and intercession in the garden?

VISITING WITH GOD

The practical side of worship and intercession has to do with *time*—when to pray; *posture*—how to pray; and *content*—what to include during visits with the Father.

All of us will find different parts of the day best for our spiritual disciplines. I am a morning person; but one of my closest friends tells me that he finds the evening hours best. Whereas I begin the day in prayer, he ends it that way. Neither of us has airtight arguments for his choice; I think it is a matter of individual rhythms. Daniel of Babylon solved the problem by being a morning and an evening person—and a noontime person too.

When I come to the morning hour, I find it virtually impossible to enter into worship or intercession the moment I come to my private place of solitude. Remember the out-of-breath principle? Praying with a fully active mind fresh from a host of conversations and decisions is difficult, if not impossible. To pray meaningfully, the mind has to be slowed down to a reflective pace.

In order to make this happen, I often begin by reading or writing in my journal. This sort of thing will slowly convince my mind that I am really serious about spiritual exercise, and so it is less liable to rebel when I turn toward prayer.

Is there a prime posture for prayer? Probably not, although some would like to make us think so. In the biblical cultures, people were most likely to stand while they prayed. However the very word *prayer* from the Old Testament means to prostrate oneself, and that may mean at times full length upon the floor.

Friends of A. W. Tozer, a great man of prayer in our time, tell me that he had a pair of coveralls in the closet in his study. When he came to the moments of prayer in his day, he put them on and stretched out upon the hard floor. The coveralls, of course, prevented him from getting his dress clothes dirty. The Muslim posture for prayer is worth trying. This is done by kneeling and then leaning forward until one's forehead is touching the floor. I have found that when I am tired, the Muslim posture helps me to be mentally and spiritually alert.

Sometimes I pray while pacing back and forth in my study; on other occasions I am content simply to sit. The point is that prayer can be carried on in all different postures—and perhaps it is best to assume all of them from one time to another.

Serious intercessors keep prayer lists. Although I am not implying that I call myself a serious intercessor, I do keep one, and it is—as I have said—in the rear of my journal. There I can review my chief concerns as I pray. It's the only way I know of making sure that those for whom God has given me a burden are responsibly lifted up as an expression of my love and caring.

THE CONTENT OF PRAYER

What should we pray about? Take a look at an excerpt from the prayers of Samuel Logan Brengle, an evangelist of the Salvation Army at the beginning of our century:

> Keep me, O Lord, from waxing mentally and spiritually dull and stupid. Help me to keep the physical, mental, and spiritual fibre of the athlete, of the man who denies himself daily and takes up his cross and follows Thee. Give me good success in my work, but hide pride from me. Save me from the self-complacency that so frequently accompanies success and prosperity. Save me from the spirit of sloth, of self-indulgence, as physical infirmities and decay creep upon me.[6]

No wonder Brengle was effective. He knew how and what to pray for. There was nothing held back, even in a short piece of intercession like this one. Having recorded this prayer, Brengle's biographer adds: "Thus praying daily and hourly, the prophet kept his passion hot and his eye single, even as he came down the decline."

6. C. W. Hall, *Samuel Logan Brengle: Portrait of a Prophet* (Chicago: Salvation Army Supply & Purchasing Dept., 1933), p. 237.

ADORATION

In our spiritual disciplines when we visit with the Father in the inner garden, adoration ought to be the first item on the worship agenda.

How can we worship in prayer? By first reflecting upon who God is and thanking Him for the things He has revealed about Himself. To worship in prayer is to allow our spirits to feast upon what God has revealed concerning His acts in the distant and recent past, and what He has told us about Himself. Slowly, as we review these things in a spirit of thanksgiving and recognition, we can sense our spirits beginning to expand, to take in the broader reality of God's presence and being. Slowly our consciousness is able to accept the fact that the universe about us is not closed or limited, but is in fact as expansive as the Creator meant for it to be. As we enter into worship we remind ourselves of how great He is.

CONFESSION

In the light of God's majesty, we are called to an honesty about ourselves: what we are by contrast. This is the second aspect of prayer: confession. Spiritual discipline calls for a regular acknowledgement of our true nature and the specific acts and attitudes of the recent past that have not been pleasurable to God as He has sought our fellowship and our obedience.

"God be merciful to me a sinner" is an abbreviated version of the prayer of confession. We need the daily humbling experience of being broken before God as we face up to our imperfection, our propensity to seek evil ways. What has startled me as a Christian has been the constant awareness of new levels of sin that I had not spotted within myself before.

Some years ago, when Gail and I bought the old abandoned New Hampshire farm we now call Peace Ledge, we found the site where we wished to build our country home strewn with rocks and boulders. It was going to take a lot of hard work to clear it all out so there could be grass and plants. The whole family went to work on the clearing process. The first phase of the clearing project was easy. The big boulders went fast. And when they were gone, we began to see that there were a lot of smaller rocks that had to go too. And so we cleared the area again. But when we had cleared the site of the boulders and rocks, we noticed all of the stones and pebbles we had not seen before. This was much harder, more tedious work. But we stuck to it, and there came a day when the soil was ready for planting grass.

Our private lives are much like that field was. When I first began to follow Christ seriously, He pointed out many major behavior and attitude patterns that, like boulders, had to be removed. And as the years went by, many of those great big boulders did indeed get removed. But when they began to disappear, I discovered a whole new layer of action and attitude in my life that I had not previously seen. But Christ saw them and rebuked them one by one. The removal process began again. Then I reached that point in my Christian life where Christ and I were dealing with stones and pebbles. They are too numerous to imagine, and as far as I can see, for the rest of my days on earth I will be working with the many stones and pebbles in my life. Every day at spiritual discipline time, there is likely to be a new stab at the clearing process.

But I must not leave this story without noting something else. Every spring at Peace Ledge, after the frost is out of the ground, we find that new stones and boulders appear around our country home. They have been beneath the surface of the ground, working their way up. And at their appointed times, one by one, they show up. Some of them are very frustrating to deal with because they look small until we try to remove them. And only then do we discover that there is more to those boulders than meets the eye.

My sinfulness is exactly the same. It consists of stones, pebbles, and boulders that come to the surface one by one. And the man or woman who ignores the daily experience of confession in spiritual discipline will soon be overwhelmed by them. I understand why the apostle Paul at an advanced age would call himself the "chief of sinners." Even while in jail facing the end of his life, he was still removing pebbles and boulders.

I smile at young believers who tell me that they are discouraged because of all the sin they see in their lives. The fact that they can at least see and feel repelled by that sin shows they are actually growing. There are too many people claiming to be followers of Christ who lost sight of their own sinfulness years ago. If they attend worship on Sunday, they leave without ever having had the experience of brokenness and repentance before God that indicates true worship. This leads to substandard Christianity.

E. Stanley Jones writes of the importance of confession in our spiritual disciplines:

> I know that there are certain mental and emotional and moral and spiritual attitudes that are anti-health: anger, resentments, fear, worry, desire to dominate, self-preoccupation, guilts, sexual impurity, jealousy, a lack of creative activity, inferiorities, a lack of love. These are the twelve apostles of ill health. *So in prayer I've learned to surrender these things to Jesus Christ as they appear.* I once asked Dr. Kagawa: "What is prayer?" And he answered: "Prayer is self-surrender." I agree. It is primarily self-surrender, blanket surrender, day by day. It is all we know and all we don't know. "All we don't know" covers the unfolding future and involves problems as they arise. So in prayer if any of these twelve things arise, and they do arise, for no one is free from the suggestion of any one of them, I've learned how to deal with them: not to fight them, but to surrender them to Jesus Christ, and say, "Now, Lord, you have this."[7]

THE MINISTRY OF INTERCESSION

The great prayer warriors all seem to agree: that intercession can begin only after we have fully worshiped. Having put ourselves in touch with the living God, we are prepared to pray with what Thomas Kelly called "the eyes of Heaven."

Old Commissioner Brengle was a man of prayer. His biographer writes:

> At prayer, he was a study in communion. It was his habit, except for those periods when he was too ill, to get out of bed between four and five o'clock in the morning and devote at least a full hour before breakfast to communion with his Lord. Dr. Hayes, whose book, "The Heights of Christian Devotion" carries these dedicatory words: "To Commissioner Samuel Logan Brengle, A Man of Prayer," gives us this glimpse:

7. E. Stanley Jones, *Song of Ascents* (Nashville: Abingdon, 1968), p. 337.

"When Brengle has been a guest in my home, I often have found him on his knees with his open Bible on the bed or chair before him, reading his Bible through in that way and saying that the attitude helped him to turn all he read into personal petition: 'O Lord, help me to do this, or not to do that. Help me to be like this man, or to avoid this error.'"[8]

When worship has been completed, intercession can begin. Intercession usually means prayer on behalf of others. It is the greatest single ministry, in my opinion, that the Christian is privileged to have. And perhaps the most difficult.

Have you ever noticed that most faithful intercessors seem to be older people? Why? One reason may be that they have had to simplify their activities. But also note that older people may have become aware that intercession is much more effective than hours of unprayerful activity. And of course, experience through trial and error has taught them the wisdom of leaning on the reliable strength of God.

I have set out in the last few years to master the ministry of intercession for the sake of ministry to others. The progress is slow. Perhaps it is the greatest challenge of my private world.

The greater the spiritual authority and responsibility a person has, the more important it is that he develop intercessory capacities. That takes time and the sort of discipline many of us find difficult.

I think this is what the apostles, the leaders of the early congregation at Jerusalem, were getting at in Acts 6, when they asked for associates to take on the tasks of ministering to the widows and orphans so that they could "give ourselves to prayer and to the preaching of the Word of God." Note what comes first on the priority list of these busy, busy men. They were starting to miss prayer and were quite nervous about the situation.

Intercession literally means to stand between two parties and plead the case of one to the other. Is there a greater example of intercession than the prayerful work of Moses, who gave himself to frequent strenuous petition on behalf of the wayward people of Israel?

8. C. W. Hall, *Portrait of a Prophet*, p. 185.

For whom do we normally intercede? If married, for our spouses and children, obviously. But, intercession also means widening the circle to take in close friends, those for whom God has made us responsible, the men and women with whom we work, and those in our congregations and neighborhoods whose personal needs are known to us.

My intercessory list includes many Christian leaders and organizations. There are many whom I know and like; but I must confess that I do not have much more than an occasional prayer burden for them. By contrast, there are some whose needs and pressures are very real to me, and I hold them before the Lord in my intercessory exercise every day. They find it of immense encouragement to hear me say, "I pray for you every day." Being responsible for a certain amount of Christian leadership myself, I have learned how supportive it feels to know that there is a handful of people who hold me before the throne of God in intercession every day.

Intercession means that we must take into account the mandate for world evangelization. In order to systematically pray around the world, I have divided up the continents in such a way that I can pray each day for one of them: Sunday, Latin America; Monday, Central America; Tuesday, North America; Wednesday, Europe; Thursday, Africa; Friday, Asia; and Saturday, the nations of the Pacific. In each area I include intercession for the national church, for missionaries with whom I am acquainted, and for the terrible suffering people are facing.

We are encouraged to bring our own petitions or requests before the Lord. Somehow I feel that these ought to come last in our prayer activity, but that is purely an opinion. I am thinking of matters in and about my personal life where it seems best to ask God for wisdom and supply. I have struggled with how much I should ask God for (some say everything) and how much He assumes we will handle ourselves. I don't know that I have a good answer to this. I discover as I grow in my faith that I am constrained to ask less and less for myself and more and more for others. And my personal requests tend to be more and more for resources and abilities that would be more of benefit for others.

The garden within our private world cannot remain uncultivated for long before it becomes infested with the sort of
growth that makes it uninviting, both to the indwelling Lord
and to us ourselves. When neglected for long, it becomes more
like a dump than a garden. And then we have to rely upon
external sources of strength and direction to keep moving
ahead.

That was the reason for Howard Rutledge's struggle in the
North Viet Nam prison camp. By God's grace, he testifies, he
made it through. But he never forgot what it is like to face
such an ordeal when one's private world of the spirit has been
left generally uncultivated.

A well-known Christian personality of our century, Eric
Liddell, the Olympic champion runner who was the hero of
the movie *Chariots of Fire*, had a remarkably different experience in a prison in North China during World War II. His
biographer speaks of the high esteem with which Liddell was
held in the Weinsen Camp. And what was the secret of his
extraordinary leadership power, his joy, and his integrity in
the midst of enormous hardship? The biographer quotes a
woman who was in the camp at the time and with her husband
knew Liddell well:

> What was his secret? Once I asked him, but I really knew already,
> for my husband was in his dormitory and shared the secret with
> him. Every morning about 6 am, with curtains tightly drawn to
> keep in the shining of our peanut-oil lamp, lest the prowling sen-
> tries would think someone was trying to escape, he used to climb
> out of his top bunk, past the sleeping forms of his dormitory
> mates. Then, at the small Chinese table, the two men would sit
> close together with the light just enough to illumine their Bibles
> and notebooks. Silently they read, prayed, thought about what
> should be done. *Eric was a man of prayer not only at set times—*
> though he did not like to miss a prayer meeting or communion
> service when such could be arranged. *He talked to God all the
> time, naturally, as one can who enters the "School of Prayer" to
> learn this way of inner discipline.* He seemed to have no weighty
> mental problems: his life was grounded in God, in faith, and in
> trust.[9]

9. Sally Magnusson, *The Flying Scotsman* (New York: Quartet Books,
1981), p. 165.

To bring order to our private worlds is to cultivate the garden as Liddell did. From such exercises, according to the writer of the Proverbs (4:23), comes a heart out of which flows life-giving energy.

At eighty years of age, bed-ridden with a stroke that impaired his speech and paralyzed his writing hand, E. Stanley Jones would ask himself: Can I handle this crisis? His answer: Absolutely. "The innermost strands are the strongest. I need no outer props to hold up my faith."

Sector Five

Memo to the Disorganized:

If my private world is in order, it will be because I have chosen to press Sabbath peace into the rush and routine of my daily life in order to find the rest God prescribed for Himself and all of humanity.

14

Rest Beyond Leisure

William Wilberforce, a committed Christian, was a member of the English Parliament in the early years of the nineteenth century. As a politician he was noted for his vigorous leadership in convincing Parliament to pass a historic bill outlawing slavery in the British Empire. It was no mean feat. In fact, it may have been one of the greatest and most courageous acts of statesmanship in the history of democracy.

It took Wilberforce almost twenty years to construct the coalition of lawmakers that eventually passed the anti-slavery measure. It required detailed documentation of the injustices and cruelties of slavery, persuading lawmakers who did not want to offend the interests of big business, and standing strong against a host of political enemies who would have loved to see Wilberforce fall.

Wilberforce's spiritual strength and moral courage had to be immense. We learn something of the source of that strength and courage from an incident that occurred in 1801, some years before the anti-slavery measure was passed.

Lord Addington had led his party into power, and as the new prime minister he had begun to form a new cabinet. The central issue of the day in England was peace; Napoleon was terrorizing Europe, and the concern was whether or not England could stay out of war. Wilberforce was rumored to be among the candidates for a cabinet post, and because of the peace policy he found himself most anxious to gain the appointment. Garth Lean, one of Wilberforce's more recent biographers, tells the story.

> It did not take long for Wilberforce to become preoccupied with the possibility of the appointment. For days it grabbed at his conscious mind, forcing aside everything else. By his own admission he had "risings of ambition," and it was crippling his soul.[1]

But there was a disciplined check and balance to Wilberforce's life, and in this particular situation that routine became indispensable. As Lean says, "Sunday brought the cure." For there came a regular time in Wilberforce's private world every week when he *rested*.

The Christian politician's journal tells the story best, in its entry at the end of that week of furious fantasizing and temptations to politic for position: "Blessed be to God for the day of rest and religious occupation wherein *earthly things assume their true size. Ambition is stunted*" (italics added).

Wilberforce's check and balance to a busy life was Sabbath; he had come to understand genuine rest. Wilberforce had discovered that the person who establishes a block of time for Sabbath rest on a regular basis is most likely to keep all of life in proper perspective and remain free of burnout and breakdown.

Not everyone in Wilberforce's public world held to that secret; workaholism and frantic busyness occurred in that day as it does today. About William Pitt, for example, Wilberforce wrote: "Poor fellow, he never schools his mind *by a cessation from political ruminations*, the most blinding, hardening and souring of all others." Of two other politicians who both took their own lives, Wilberforce wrote, "With peaceful Sundays, the strings would never have snapped as they did from overtension."

There can be little order in the private world of the human being when there is no appreciation for the meaning and pursuit of genuine rest, a *cessation*, as Wilberforce called it, in

1. Garth Lean, *God's Politician* (London: Darton, Longman & Todd, 1980), p. 89.

the routines of our times. From the beginning of all history, it has been an axiom at the base of healthy living; unfortunately, it is a principle badly misunderstood by those whose lives are driven to achievement and acquisition.

WE NEED REST

I get the feeling we are a tired generation. Evidence of that fatigue abounds in a multitude of articles about health problems related to overwork and exhaustion. *Workaholism* is a modern word. No matter how hard we are willing to work in our competitive world, there always seems to be someone willing to put in a few more hours than we are.

What is strange about our general fatigue as a people is the fact that we are such a leisure-oriented society. We actually have what is called a leisure industry, and it is among the most profitable in our economy. Whole companies, organizations, and retail chain stores are committed to providing the goods with which people can pursue fun and good times.

We probably have more time for leisure than we ever had before. The five-day workweek is, after all, a relatively new innovation in history; we have moved away from the farm, where there was always more work to do; we can leave work behind if we want and head for leisure. So why is there so much exhaustion and fatigue today? Is it real? Imagined? Or is the contemporary form of exhaustion evidence that we no longer understand genuine rest, which is different from the pursuit of leisure?

There is a biblical view of rest that needs to be uncovered and examined. In fact, the Bible reveals God Himself to be the first "rester." "On the seventh day, He rested. . . ." An even more enlightening comment is made by Moses in Exodus 31:17: "In six days the Lord made heaven and earth, but on the seventh day, He ceased from labor, and was refreshed." The literal translation suggests the phrase "He refreshed Himself."

Does God indeed need to rest? Of course not! But did God choose to rest? Yes. Why? Because God subjected creation to a rhythm of rest and work that He revealed by observing the rhythm Himself, as a precedent for everyone else. In this way, He showed us a key to order in our private worlds.

This rest was not meant to be a luxury, but rather a *necessity* for those who want to have growth and maturity. Since we have not understood that rest is a necessity, we have perverted its meaning, substituting for the rest that God first demonstrated things called leisure or amusement. These do not bring any order at all to the private world. Leisure and amusement may be enjoyable, but they are to the private world of the individual like cotton candy to the digestive system. They provide a momentary lift, but they will not last.

I am not by any means critical of the pursuit of fun-filled moments, diversion, laughter, or recreation. I am proposing that these alone will not restore the soul in the way that we crave. Although they may provide a sort of momentary rest for the body, they will not satisfy the deep need for rest within the private world.

Years ago there was a famous ad campaign for a liniment, which promised that the product would penetrate deeply into sore muscles, bringing relief from aches and pains. Sabbath rest penetrates to the deepest levels of fatigue in the inner, private world. This fatigue is rarely touched by any of the modern amusements.

THE MEANING OF SABBATH REST

CLOSING THE LOOP

When God rested, He looked upon His work, enjoyed its completed appearance, and then reflected upon its meaning. "And God saw that it was good." This shows us the first of the three principles of genuine rest. God gave His work meaning and acknowledged its completion. In so doing, He taught us that there is a necessary exercise of appreciation and dedication for our routines.

High-tech systems planners like to use the phrase "closing the loop" to describe the completion of a phase in an electrical circuit. They also use the phrase when they want to say that a task has been completed or that every person in a project has been informed or consulted.

So you could say that on the seventh day, God closed the loop on His primary creation activity. He closed it by resting and looking back upon it to survey what had been accomplished.

This rest then is, first of all, a time of looking backward, of loop-closing. We gaze upon our work and ask questions like: What does my work mean? For whom did I do this work? How well was the work done? Why did I do this? and What results did I expect, and what did I receive?

To put it another way, the rest God instituted was meant first and foremost to cause us to *interpret* our work, to *press meaning into it, to make sure we know to whom it is properly dedicated.*

Brother Lawrence was a cook in a monastery. He learned to press meaning into virtually every action of his day. Note his capacity to see not only meaning but also purpose in his labor:

> I turn my little omelette in the pan for the love of God. When it is finished, if I have nothing to do, I prostrate myself on the ground and worship my God, who gave me this grace to make it, after which I arise happier than a king. When I can do nothing else, it is enough to have picked up a straw for the love of God. People look for ways of learning how to love God. They hope to attain it by I know not how many different practices. They take much trouble to abide in His presence by varied means. Is it not a shorter and more direct way to do everything for the love of God, to make use of all the tasks one's lot in life demands to show him that love, and to maintain his presence within by the communion of our heart with his? There is nothing complicated about it. One has only to turn to it honestly and simply.[2]

I am sure that most of us desire periods of time like that. The average worker has a desperate need to feel that his work means something, has significance, and is appreciated. But, while we crave that assurance, we do not see the importance of taking time to gain it. A busyness, a frantic pace sets in, and we delay our quest for meaning and interpretation; before long, we have learned to get along without it. We lose sight of the question, What's this all for? We become content to allow

2. Brother Lawrence, *The Practice of the Presence of God*, trans. E. M. Blaiklock (Nashville: Thomas Nelson, 1982), p. 85.

the meaning value of our work to be computed merely in the amount on our paychecks. Few people appreciate how dry and barren this leaves our private world.

A man I like very much was recently terminated by his company after twenty-two years of service. The economy had forced an across-the-board cutback, and his job was considered non-essential to the company's survival. He was out!

My friend was convinced that he would be hired by another company in the same field within a matter of days. After all, he told me, he had numerous connections, a profit-making record, and long term service. He was not worried, he said.

But several months passed with no offers. The "connections" dried up; no one responded to his feelers or to his resumés. He was reduced to sitting at home waiting for the phone to ring.

One day, after those many torturous months, he said to me, "This whole thing has forced me to do a lot of hard thinking. I've given myself to this career of mine for years, and look what it's gotten me. What was all this for anyway? Boy, have I gotten my eyes opened up."

Opened up to what? My friend is a fine Christian layman. But his eyes, by his own admission, had been closed to what his career had come to mean to him. What his eyes had opened up to was the fact that he had worked for years without asking what it all meant, what it was all for, and what might be the result. He had never discovered the exercise of reflection in the context of biblical rest.

A rest-less work style produces a restless person. Work that goes on month after month without a genuine pause to inquire of its meaning and purpose may swell the bank account and enhance the professional reputation. But it will drain the private world of vitality and joy. How important it is to regularly close loops on our activity.

RETURNING TO THE ETERNAL TRUTHS

There is a second way biblical rest restores order to the private world. True rest is happening when we pause regularly amidst daily routines to sort out the truths and commitments by which we are living.

We are daily the objects of a bombardment of messages competing for our loyalties and labors. We are pushed and pulled in a thousand different directions, asked to make decisions and value judgments, to invest our resources and our time. By what standard of truth do we make these decisions?

God meant for His people to take a day each week in which this question was firmly dealt with. And in fact, He caused them to set aside a series of annual feast days during which major themes of eternal truth and divine action could be recalled and celebrated. You could call it a recalibration of the spirit.

Separating out the truths that are central to life is essential when one remembers that, according to Jeremiah, the heart is deceitful. We are vulnerable at all times to distortions of the truth, to persuasions that the true is really false and the false really true. Remember the words of the hymnwriter:

> Prone to wander, Lord, I feel it;
> Prone to leave the God I love. . .
> (Robert Robinson)

The hymn reflects upon the inexorable inward drift that must be regularly checked by measuring our thoughts and values against the eternal truths that have been revealed through the Scripture and the mighty acts of God.

The Jewish theologian Abraham Joshua Heschel looked at rest in the Sabbath tradition and wrote:

> The meaning of the Sabbath is to celebrate time rather than space. Six days a week, we live under the tyranny of things of space; on the Sabbath we try to become attuned to holiness in time. It is a day on which we are called upon to share what is eternal in time, to turn from the results of creation to the mystery of creation; from the world of creation to the creation of the world.[3]

We need to ask ourselves, Is this happening in my own private world?

---

3. Abraham Heschel, *The Earth Is the Lord's and The Sabbath* (two books published as one, New York: Harper Torchbooks, 1966), p. 10.

The clapboards of our New Hampshire home expand and contract in response to temperature extremes. The result is that some nails work loose and have to be pounded back in to regain a snug hold. This "repounding" is what happens during a genuine rest period, be it in the privacy of that quiet day or in the midst of a congregation while we worship the living God.

One of the great joys of repeating the traditional creeds of the Christian church is that it gives us an opportunity to re-affirm the central truths of God's revelation. As we say, "I believe . . ." we begin to hammer back the nails of our convictions and commitments. And we separate those beliefs out from what we choose not to believe.

The same thing happens when we sing grand old hymns and pray certain prayers. The nails are being pounded back in, and order is being restored to a drifting spirit in our private worlds. Reaffirmations occur on that special rest day, if we take time in private for reading, meditating, and reflecting.

My wife shares with me an entry in her journal on this very subject:

> A glorious Lord's Day. Have been reading at length about the Sabbath. Feel more and more strongly that I've not fully utilized God's command to rest.
>
> It's not a rule that restricts but it is a rule that liberates. For He made me to need rest. And physically and mentally we are freed to better performance if we live within His "design specifications." And it is a day of reminding us who God is. Every seventh day I need to come back to the fixed Center.
>
> Don Stephenson remarked today that for him and others Sunday is just that—a day to come back to the straight edge and be encouraged to go back to the "mire."

I would propose that we need to ask hard questions, both of ourselves and of our churches, concerning whether or not the sort of rest that reaffirms truth is actually happening. It is possible for Christians and their churches to become so busy carrying on programs—for whatever good purpose—that the worship-rest necessary to the private world never happens.

Thus, rest is not only a looking back at the meaning of my work and the path I have so recently walked in my life; but is also a refreshing of my belief and commitment to Christ. It is a fine tuning of my inner navigational instruments so that I can make my way through the world for another week.

DEFINING OUR MISSION

If the first two meanings centered on what was past and present, this one centers on the future. When we rest in the biblical sense, we affirm our intentions to pursue a Christ-centered tomorrow. We ponder where we are headed in the coming week, month or year. We define our intentions and make our dedications.

General George Patton demanded that his men know and be able to articulate exactly what the current mission was. "What is your mission?" he would frequently ask. The definition of the mission was the most important piece of information a soldier could carry into combat. Based on that knowledge, he could make his decisions and implement the plan. That is exactly what happens when I pursue biblical rest. I take a hard look at my mission. And it has taught me to make a small pause even in my spiritual disciplines each morning to ask the question, What is my mission today? Not to regularly ask this question is to leave yourself open to mistakes of judgment and direction.

Jesus often withdrew to seek solitude. While others were lulled to the rest of sleep, Jesus was drawn to the rest of gaining strength and direction for His next phase of mission. No wonder He met every encounter with a fresh burst of wisdom. No wonder He had ample courage not to fight back, not to defend Himself. His spirit was always rested, His private world ordered. Without this kind of rest our private world will always be strained and disordered.

CHOOSING TO REST

One of the noted vicars of the Church of England was Charles Simeon, of Holy Trinity Church in Cambridge. For more than fifty years he preached from its pulpit, and the people crowded the sanctuary, standing in the aisles to hear him.

Simeon was a fellow at Kings College, and he lived in apartments that overlooked the courtyard in the college complex. His second-floor dwellings provided him an exclusive opening out to the roof where he would often walk, one of his physical forms of rest, while he talked with God. That rooftop became known as Simeon's walk.

A busy and brilliant man, Simeon was in touch with students at the colleges in Cambridge, with a large congregation, and with church and missionary leaders around the world. He wrote (in longhand) literally thousands of letters, edited fifty books of his own sermons, and served as one of the founders of several major missionary organizations. But he never ceased to find time for the rest that his private world demanded.

A sample of his private exercises can be found in this entry to his journal, recorded by Hugh Hopkins, a Simeon biographer.

> I spent this day as I have for these 43 last years, as a day of humiliation; having increased need of such season every year I live.

Hopkins writes:

> Self-humiliation for Charles Simeon consisted not of belittling the gifts that God had given him or pretending that he was a man of no account, or exaggerating the sins of which he was very conscious. He went about it by consciously bringing himself into the presence of God, dwelling thoughtfully on his majesty and glory, magnifying the mercy of his forgiveness and the wonder of his love. These were the things that humbled him—not so much his own sinfulness but God's incredible love.[4]

Simeon enjoyed a lifelong effectiveness under enormous strain. I have no doubt that a large part of his secret of endurance was his deliberate and disciplined pursuit of Sabbath rest.

4. Hugh Evan Hopkins, *Charles Simeon of Cambridge* (Grand Rapids: Eerdmans, 1977), pp. 155–56.

For the Jew, the Sabbath was first of all a day. A day set aside in obedience to God. The law forbade work of any kind, allowing only the sort of observances such as we have already reviewed. Christians have little idea of how special the Sabbath was to pious Jews. We would do well to listen and hear what they think. An Israeli tourist brochure tells us that one rabbi wrote of Sabbath:

> Make the Sabbath an eternal monument of the knowledge and sanctification of God, both in the center of your busy public life and in the peaceful retreat of your domestic hearth. For six days cultivate the earth and rule it. . . . But the seventh is the Sabbath of the Lord thy God. . . . Let [a man] therefore realize that the Creator of old is the living God of today, [that He] watches every man and every human effort, to see how man uses or abuses the world loaned to him and the forces bestowed upon him, and that He is the sole architect to Whom every man has to render an account of his week's labors.

What is important behind these statements is the Jewish awareness of a unique pace to Sabbath. Routines are to stop; labor is to cease. Even the homemaker in the pious Jewish family is to refrain from cooking or menial tasks. Food is prepared before Sabbath begins so that she also can enjoy the fruit of the special rest day. This is a far cry from the incredible, filled up, pressurized day many evangelical Christians tend to make of their "day of rest."

Sabbath is first of all a day. In our Christian tradition we have chosen to make that day not the seventh, as the Jew does, but the first day of the week, in recognition of the resurrection of Christ. But having made that choice, what have we done with our day—this time that God gave as a special gift?

A layman with whom I worship every week said to me after one particularly long Sunday of church activity, "I'm sure glad that there is only one rest day per week, I'd burn out if we had to go through two 'days of rest' like this every seven days."

His humor conveys a serious charge against many Christian leaders and churches who have turned Sunday into a day of unrest, perhaps for some the most tension-filled day of the week.

But Sabbath is more than just a day. It is a principle of rest along the lines of the three dimensions I have already mentioned. And what might happen should we choose the peace of Sabbath rest rather than the fun of secular leisure?

First, Sabbath rest means worship with the Christian family. In proper worship we will have a chance to exercise all three aspects that lead to the rest of our private worlds: looking backward, upward, and ahead. Such worship is nonnegotiable to the person committed to walking with God.

I am moved by the words of Luke who describes the Sabbath discipline of Jesus: "And He came *to Nazareth, where He had been brought up; and as was His custom, He entered the synagogue on the Sabbath*" (Luke 4:16, italics added). One never sees Christ slipping away from the public worship of the Father.

But, second, Sabbath means a deliberate acceptance of personal rest and tranquility within the individual life. Sabbath means a rest that brings peace into the private world. As Christ pressed stillness into a storm, order into a being of a demon-possessed maniac, health into a desperately sick woman, and life into a dead friend, so He seeks to press peace into the harried private world of the man or woman who has been in the marketplace all week. But there is a condition. We must accept this peace as a gift and take the time to receive it.

As a pastor, I have long felt that Sunday was anything but Sabbath rest for my wife and me. It was many years into my Christian adulthood before I realized that I had been robbing myself of a necessary form of restoration. The fact was that I needed some sort of Sabbath for my own private world, and I wasn't getting it. When I looked at my Sundays, it seemed impossible to think that I would ever enjoy Sabbath's rejuvenating gift. How could I preach three Sunday morning sermons and a frequent evening sermon, as well as be available throughout the day to the people of my congregation, and expect to be restored? Rarely did a Sunday end without Gail and me being on the verge of exhaustion. Day of rest indeed!

What to do? A few years ago, the Grace Chapel congregation was gracious enough to give me a four-month sabbatical leave. Rather than go off to a university to study, I chose to go to New Hampshire, where we built Peace Ledge. The outstanding experience of those four months was the silence and peace we discovered on Sundays.

Although I enjoyed the construction of Peace Ledge immensely, I promised myself that I would do no work on the Lord's Day. Thus, when Sunday came, we spent a few early morning hours reading, thinking, and praying. And then we went to a local church where we could worship. We did not know many of the people, but we tried to throw ourselves into the worship and draw from the prayers, the hymns, and the sermon food for our spirits. We made it a time of affirming our convictions, thanking God for blessings, and committing ourselves to the coming week in which we would try to reflect the honor of the Lord.

Our Sunday afternoons during the four months were quiet hours for walks in the woods, deep conversation, and a searching process as we evaluated our spiritual disciplines and Christian progress. It was a marvelously restful Sabbath experience for us; I had never known what it could be like before that time.

We were hooked on Sabbaths when we returned from our sabbatical. But suddenly it was back to sermons, and counseling, and programming. Business as usual on Sunday. We felt robbed! And so it was that we decided *our* Sabbath would be another day of the week. We were not going to miss God's gift! On Sundays, we would try to help others enjoy their Sabbaths. But for us the peace normally reserved for that day would have to happen at some other time. And that was fine.

Sabbath for Gail and me became Thursday. To the extent that we could achieve it, we budgeted that day of the week for rest in our private worlds. It meant total withdrawal from our congregation whenever possible, even laying aside the routines of our home if we could. We learned that if we were going to be useful to those associated with us in ministry, to our children, and to the congregation, we would have to jealously guard this opportunity for spiritual restoration.

There is no legalism here—rather a freedom to accept a gift. Frankly, I think some have destroyed the joy of Sabbath, as did the Pharisees, by surrounding it with prescriptive laws and precedents. That is not our Sabbath. Our Sabbath was made for us, given to us by God. Its purpose is worship and restoration, and whatever it takes to make that happen, we will do.

It is important to say that we probably could not have pursued Sabbath rest as easily when our children were young and needed more constant attention. And it is also important to say, as Gail often observes, that we do our people a favor by withdrawing from them for rest. For when we return, we have something to offer that God probably could not have given us in any other atmosphere.

Obviously, every Thursday could not be budgeted for Sabbath. But, we discovered that if we made a regular attempt at such a discipline, the results were tremendous. Our private worlds were indeed substantially reordered. The most astounding discovery was that I felt not only rested but able to use the times of other days in a far more effective fashion.

What had happened, much to my amazement, was that by bringing this restful order to my private world through proper Sabbath observance, I was able to impact my public world in the days that followed with much greater wisdom and judgment.

I believe that Sabbath rest may mean a day a week. But it can happen at any time, in large and small doses, when we choose to set aside an hour or more for the pursuit of intimacy with God. All of us need a "Simeon's walk."

But let me be quick to underscore that this rest, which is Sabbathlike, ought to be a fixed allocation in the budgeting of our time. We do not rest because our work is done; we rest because God commanded it and created us to have a need for it.

That is important to think about, because our current view of rest and leisure denies that principle. Most of us think of resting as something we do *after* our work is done. But Sabbath is not something that happens after. It may in fact be something that is pursued *before*. If we assume that this rest comes only after work is complete, many of us are in trouble, for we have jobs where the work is never finished. And that in part is why some of us rarely rest; never finishing our work,

we do not think to take the time for Sabbath peace and restoration.

I had to learn to pursue Sabbath rest without a sense of
guilt. I had to realize that there was nothing wrong with laying aside other work for the purpose of enjoying God's gift of
special time. Thus, Sabbaths have gone into our calendars
with regularity. They are planned weeks in advance, along
with other priorities. And when someone has proposed a supper, a ball game, or a committee meeting on a day set aside for
the reordering of our private worlds, my wife and I have simply said, "Sorry, we have a commitment on that day. It's Sabbath for us."

It was this sort of discipline that enabled William Wilberforce to overcome the consuming thrust of ambition that had
crippled his private world for so many days. Having reached
the day of rest, he slipped back into that center where God
was in full control. He saw things in their true size, "ambition
is stunted," he wrote.

One wonders what would have happened if Wilberforce had
not had that Sabbath check and balance to face his ambitious
nature. Would he have been deterred from his call to lead England away from slavery? Probably. You have to believe that in
taking Sabbath, he was able to detect a deviation from his
original sense of purpose and, just in time, regain the right
course. Because he got back on track, the great landmark
achievement of abolition was his to claim.

The world and the church need genuinely *rested* Christians:
Christians who are regularly refreshed by true Sabbath rest,
not just leisure or time off. When a godly rest is achieved, you
will see just how tough and resilient Christians can actually
be.

Memo to the Disorganized:

If my private world is in order, it will be because I have made a deliberate decision to begin the "ordering" process . . . Now!

Epilogue:
The Spinning Wheel

One of the celebrated heroes of our century has been Mohandas Gandhi, the Indian leader who sparked the flame of independence for his country. Those who have read his biographies or who have seen his story so brilliantly told upon the screen are often impressed with the tranquil spirit that "India's George Washington" displayed.

Serenity? We see Gandhi among the most poverty-ridden people of Indian cities, where death and disease are rampant. He touches them, offers a word of hope, provides a gentle smile. But a day later the same man is found in palaces and government buildings, where he negotiates with the most clever men of his age. And the question arises: how did he manage to span the gap between the two extremes of people and circumstances?

How could Gandhi maintain his private sense of order, his appropriate humility, and his base wisdom and judgment? How did he avoid losing his own identity and spirit of conviction as he moved between those enormous extremes? Where did the emotional and spiritual force come from?

Perhaps the beginning of an answer to those questions lies in Gandhi's fascination with the simple spinning wheel. The wheel seems to have always been at the center of his life. Gandhi appears to have often returned from public exposure to his humble dwellings where he would, in Indian fashion, sit upon the floor and engage in the simple act of spinning the wool from which his clothes were made.

What was he trying to do? Was this merely part of a plan to project a certain image? Was it purely a political attempt to identify with the masses, whose loyalty he held in his grasp? I would suggest that it was much, much more.

Gandhi's spinning wheel was his center of gravity in life. It was the great leveler in his human experience. When he returned from the great public moments in his life, the spinning-wheel experience restored him to his proper sense of proportion, so that he was not falsely swelled with pride due to the cheers of the people. When he withdrew from the moments of encounter with kings and government leaders, he was not tempted to think of himself in some inflated fashion when he moved to the work of the wheel.

The spinning wheel was always a reminder to Gandhi of who he was and what the practical things in life were all about. In engaging in this regular exercise, he was resisting all the forces of his public world that tried to distort who he knew himself to be.

Gandhi was by no means a Christian, but what he was doing at the wheel is an indispensable lesson for any healthy Christian. For he shows us what every man or woman who wants to move in a public world without being pressed into its mold needs to do. We, too, need the spinning-wheel experience— the ordering of our private worlds so that they are constantly restructured in strength and vitality.

As Thomas Kelly says, "We are trying to be several selves at once, without all our selves being organized by a single, mastering Life within us." Again he says, "Life is meant to be lived from a Center, a divine Center. Each one of us can live such a life of amazing power and peace and serenity, of integration and confidence and simplified multiplicity, on one condition—that is, *if we really want to.*"

And that is the condition with which we must finally deal. Do we really want order within our private worlds? Again, *do we want it?*

If it is true that actions speak louder than words, it would appear that the average Christian does not really seek an ordered private world as a top priority. It would seem that we prefer to find our human effectiveness through busyness, frantic programming, material accumulation, and rushing to various conferences, seminars, film series, and special speakers.

In short, we try to bring order to the inner world by beginning with activity in the outer one. This is exactly the opposite of what the Bible teaches us, what the great saints have shown us, and what our dismal spiritual experiences regularly prove to us.

Somewhere John Wesley is quoted as saying of life in his public world, "Though I am always in haste, I am never in a hurry, because I never undertake more work than I can go through with calmness of spirit."

One of my close associates in ministry, Bob Ludwig, is a stargazer. Occasionally he spends an evening in the countryside, where he can turn his telescope on the darkened sky. But he must leave the city in order to escape all the interfering light. Once he has left all of that behind, the picture of the sky becomes much clearer.

How do we escape such interference in order to gaze into the inner space of our private world? That question remains dangerously unanswered in too many lives. Men and women who command the leadership of large organizations and churches too often are unable to answer the question for themselves. Simple people, busy earning a living and trying to keep up with the Joneses, are wrestling with the question. It yields no easy answer—only a simple one. We escape into the space of the inner world only when we determine that it is an activity more important than anything else we do.

Although I have always believed in the priority of ordering my inner world, it has only begun to become a reality for me as I have advanced toward the middle years of my life. And now that I have grown increasingly aware of my limits, my weaknesses, and even the advance of the years toward the day when my own life shall end, I find it more possible to look within and cultivate the spinning-wheel experience, so that inner strength and spiritual vitality can become a resource.

It is at that center that we begin to see Jesus Christ in all

His majesty. There He is more than what is contained in some doctrinal statement about Him. He is more than the mushy words of some contemporary song. At the center, He commands attention as the risen Lord of life; and we are compelled to follow after Him and draw from the strength of His character and compassion.

At the center, we are appropriately awed by the splendor and majesty of God as heavenly Father. There is solemn but joyful worship; there are confession and breaking. And there is forgiveness, restoration, and assurance.

Finally, at the center, we are filled by the power and strength of God as Holy Spirit. There is a resurgence of confidence and expectancy. We receive insight and wisdom; faith that removes mountains is generated, and a love for others, even for the unlovable, begins to grow.

When we come from an experience at the spinning wheel, where all is returned to proper proportion and value, the public world can be managed and properly touched. Relationships with family and friends, with business associates, neighbors, and even enemies take on a new and healthier perspective. It becomes possible to forgive, to serve, to not seek vengeance, to be generous.

Our work will be affected by exercise at the center. Work will be given new meaning and a higher standard of excellence. Integrity and honesty will become important items of pursuit. Fear will be lost, and compassion will be gained.

Coming from the spinning-wheel experience, we are less apt to be seduced by the false promises and seductions of those out to capture the soul.

All of this and much more goes into motion when the private world is ordered first—*before* the Christian walks in the public world.

Not to do that is to invite the sinkhole syndrome. And history abounds with examples of people who own that consequence.

Today our public worlds demand a few good people who can walk among the masses and negotiate with the powerful, but never change, never capitulate, never compromise.

And how will they manage that? By pursuing the spinning-wheel experience: the retreat into the silent center where time can be ordered by priorities, where the mind can be tuned to discover God's creation, the spirit can be sharpened, and where there is the quietness of Sabbath rest. This is the private world, and when given proper attention, it comes to order.

End Pages

by Ralph W. Neighbour, Jr.

A CHINESE PROVERB

Once there was a wealthy Chinese merchant who had a beautiful ornamental garden. He had spent much time and money creating it, bringing rare plants from across the world to be displayed in his valley.

Among the imported plants was a stately clump of bamboos that grew to a gigantic size. They rose high above all the other plants, and were quite proud of their height. The bamboo plants said to each other, "We are the tallest of all the master's plants. We rise above them all!"

Day by day, they waved to the people walking on the road above the valley. Many of those who passed by did not look down to notice the lovely garden, and it irritated the clump of bamboo trees. They would ripple their fronds and rub against one another, making noises to attract the tourists.

From time to time, the master strolled through his garden, examining all the plants. He always felt a tenderness toward the ones not doing well, and would sometimes dig around them to give them more water or fertilizer.

Then a great drought came to the area. Weeks went by without any rain and the garden suffered from the lack of water. The bamboo plants observed the master visiting frequently during that time. He would go away looking very sad.

During those times, the hardy bamboo trees sought to cheer him by waving their tallest fronds and rubbing against one another to make a melodious sound. They hoped that would cheer him up!

Then the master appeared with an ax. He walked up to the bamboo trees and examined them carefully. As he did so, they swelled with pride. *"Finally!"* they said to one another, "The master has realized how valuable we are among all these smaller plants."

The master approached them and spoke: "Bamboo trees, I have need of you! You are my only hope."

Proudly they answered, "Yes, master! Many of the people who admire your garden come because of our signals. We have been the attraction that caused them to notice the garden and come down from the road above."

The master replied, "Yes, I have recognized you have done that. But that is not why I need you. You have seen all the other plants beginning to die because they have no water. I have brought this axe to cut you off at the ground. I must then lay each of you on your sides and take my sharp knife and go inside you, cutting away the partitions within. I will make a length of tubing from each of you and then join you together to make a great pipeline. There is a spring up on the mountain that is flowing with pure water. I will put one end of you in that spring, and you will bring the fluid that comes through you to water my garden. You are my only solution. Unless I do this with you, all the plants will die. *I have need of you. You are my only hope.*"

THE MASTER IS SAYING, "I HAVE NEED OF YOU!"

Consider the journey that has brought you to this point in your Christian life:

- You came to the cross, and exchanged your life with Christ. He came to reside within you.

- You began your journey, and learned that the very first activity of the Holy Spirit was to baptize you into the body of Christ.

- Your life in the cell group provided you with a sponsor, and you learned the importance of transparency with a fellow Christian.

- You journeyed through the *Year of Equipping,* learning as you went along that many of your values had to be abandoned.

183

- You experienced the high drama of helping a "Type A" unbeliever accept Jesus Christ, and you brought this baby Christian into your cell group.

- You spent many months serving on a team of three from your cell, and you learned how to relate to the hard core unbeliever who had no interest in God.

- You experienced the presence of God week by week in your cell and in your ministry to unbelievers. His power was manifested during the previous months,and you saw Him work through you and the cell members to do marvelous acts.

- You have been seasoned by your life in the cell group church, and have learned the power of the scriptures as they were presented in messages and implemented in edification times in your cell group.

Can you recall how God began to speak to you about the step you are now taking? When and where did it happen? A person like you shared this report:

For me, I began to realize how God was calling me to a new dimension of ministry as I watched the lives of our cell leaders and cell leader interns. Week by week, their love for me and their encouragement for me to complete "The Year of Equipping" showed me a servant heart in action.

The Lord began to say, "Do you not know I have chosen you to be a special vessel in my Kingdom? All I have done to you has simply been preparation for what I am going to do with you. I will now call you to lay down your life to find the greater service I have reserved for you. I want you to be like these models I have shown you. It is time for you to become a shepherd of My sheep."

Well, that was it for me! When my cell leader and zone supervisor came to ask me to pray about becoming a cell leader intern, I answered, "I have already been praying about this. I know God is calling me. The answer is 'yes!' When do I begin training?"

184

WHY THIS SECTION IS CALLED "END PAGES:"

As you come to the end of your cell leader intern training, you end the demanding schedule you have had to keep. Perhaps you have said, "This training moves so fast. Why do we not do this in ten or more weeks? Why is it compacted into eight weeks? The pace is so heavy!" Now that you are completing it, there may be value in your knowing why so many demands have been made on you.

You have been challenged to read this book and *order your private world.* Consider MacDonald's statement:

If my private world is in order, it will be because I have begun to pursue the discipline of seeing events and people through the eyes of Christ so that my prayers reflect my desire to be in alignment with His purposes and promises for them (Page 143).

The discipline of these eight weeks has been for you to *see events and people through the eyes of Christ.* Your special relationship with your Trainer, your Pastor, and your cell leader has given you insights into the way pastoral care takes place. More than just reading books or attending classes, you have been exposed to others who have modeled what your ministry will involve. Now you are at the end—*the beginning end!* Your own ministry starts now.

A TRUE STORY ...

Some years ago while studying in seminary and pastoring a church at the same time, I began to resent the many demands being made upon me by my schedule. To teach me, the Lord placed in my path a young man my own age who was going through his medical internship in a nearby hospital. His schedule was so hectic that he seldom had time to attend worship services, so I suggested we meet privately at my home to pray and share. He would call me at midnight, saying, "Are you still studying your Hebrew lesson? I am off duty and could come over if you are willing to see me."

185

When he would arrive, I sometimes discovered he had been on duty in the emergency room for 48 hours straight, snatching sleep whenever he had a few minutes of break between incoming patients. He was being stretched far beyond my own schedule!

I asked, "Why in the world do they do this to you? This is insane!"

He replied, "No, Ralph. It's part of what it takes to see if I have what it takes to be a physician. If I slip up when my mind and body are tired and make a wrong diagnosis, there are other doctors around me who can stop me from treating a patient in a way that will not cure the problem. They know I am exhausted, but expect absolute perfection from me while in that condition. Before I can become a doctor, I must prove that I will always be dependable, no matter how exhausted I might be."

YOUR ROLE AS A CELL LEADER

You are about to become a physician treating the souls of men and women! You will be the first level of pastoral care for those who look to you as their primary shepherd. A part of your training during these eight weeks has been to see if you will "stick by the stuff," or if your zeal is a rocket in the sky that will fizzle out.

You are being called to be a model to people who need to see how you deal with problems they will face in their own journeys. You are a shepherd of the sheep. You have been through "internship" in a spiritual hospital setting. You have been at the side of your cell leader in many different situations and have learned to guide the cell through its meetings.

In the weeks to come, you will gradually be given the primary leadership of the cell group. Before the six months of internship is over, your cell leader will surrender the group to your care and take a short "furlough," still being at your side for your every need.

When you are exhausted, when you feel like quitting the ministry of serving as a cell leader, remember the young doctor who fully understood why he was being put through the disciplines needed to treat patients. You are learning how *to be in alignment with His purposes and promises* for the cell members.

My Personal Covenant

Knowing that Christ has called me to the ministry of being a cell leader, I will declare Him to be Lord over all my shepherding tasks.

My body, my possessions, and my future are His to command.

I will be available to my Basic Christian Community as they face crises in their bodies, souls, and spirits. I will seek to encourage each person to deal with strongholds and find Christ's freedom.

I will seek to inspire each cell member to complete the Year of Equipping.

I will encourage the mature believers to embark on ministries to the unreached.

I will be under the guidance and counsel of my zone supervisor and zone pastor at all times.

In this spirit, I invite His Spirit to take my life and use it for His glory.

———————————————————

Name

———————————————————

Date

CELL LEADER'S JOURNAL

MacDonald writes, "I found that one practical way to learn to listen to God speak in the garden of my private world was to keep a journal. With a pencil in hand ready to write, I found that there was an expectancy, a readiness to hear anything God might wish to whisper through my reading and reflection."

The last section of this book is a place for you to journal your time with the Lord. These eight weeks of preparation to be a cell leader will be very special to you. By recording in this book the insights the Father gives to you, you will be preserving special thoughts in a special place. As you read the chapters of this book, write down the messages God speaks to you.

It is suggested that you then return to the portion of this book *you* wrote in the months ahead. Times when you may want to reflect again on what the Lord has spoken to you may be when you are discouraged and think the burden of your cell members is too heavy to bear, or when you are first meeting with a new cell leader intern who has been assigned to your care. Many of the insights you will write in these pages will be useful when sharing with him.

Keeping a record of where you have *been* will influence where you are *going!* The pages which follow have been prepared for you to use as you reflect over the chapters assigned in the book. It is assumed that you would read each section of this book at one sitting. The journal provided then gives you five days of pages to write down your thoughts as they come to you.

This period of eight weeks of training will be very busy ones. You will have classes to attend, books to read, assignments given to you by your cell leader. It is during such times of outward activity that your inner life is most important!

May the journal you write here bless and strengthen your journey outward as a messenger bearing Christ's love!

Week 1, Day 1

Reading Assignment for the Week: Preface through Chapter 2

Insights into my private world and my fellowship with Christ:

Insights into serving the cell members and unbelievers in my public world:

Insights into specific cell members or those in their *oikoses*; Actions I might take today to serve them:

Week 1, Day 2

Reading Assignment for the Week: Preface through Chapter 2

Insights into my private world and my fellowship with Christ:

Insights into serving the cell members and unbelievers in my public world:

Insights into specific cell members or those in their *oikoses* ; Actions I might take today to serve them:

Week 1, Day 3

Reading Assignment for the Week: Preface through Chapter 2

Insights into my private world and my fellowship with Christ:

Insights into serving the cell members and unbelievers in my public world:

Insights into specific cell members or those in their *oikoses* ; Actions I might take today to serve them:

Week 1, Day 4

Reading Assignment for the Week: Preface through Chapter 2

Insights into my private world and my fellowship with Christ:

Insights into serving the cell members and unbelievers in my public world:

Insights into specific cell members or those in their *oikoses* ; Actions I might take today to serve them:

Week 1, Day 5

Reading Assignment for the Week: Preface through Chapter 2

Insights into my private world and my fellowship with Christ:

Insights into serving the cell members and unbelievers in my public world:

Insights into specific cell members or those in their *oikoses* ; Actions I might take today to serve them:

Week 2, Day 1

Reading Assignment for the Week: Chapters 3-5

Insights into my private world and my fellowship with Christ:

I struggle to balance my driven nature with my spiritual journey. I return to my spiritual basis for comfort and balance. I want to be controlled by the Holy Spirit.

Insights into serving the cell members and unbelievers in my public world:

It requires time to help and reach others. I need to focus less on work to give me more time and energy to devote to people.

Insights into specific cell members or those in their *oikoses*; Actions I might take today to serve them:

Many of us are driven people. Patrice has made much progress in this balance.

Week 2, Day 2

Reading Assignment for the Week: Chapters 3-5

Insights into my private world and my fellowship with Christ:

I Need To spend more Time with Christ.

Insights into serving the cell members and unbelievers in my public world:

I will be more effective if I respond To The CAll of The God.

Insights into specific cell members or those in their *oikoses* ; Actions I might take today to serve them:

Jimmy - listening encouraging in sTudy & learning Sounding boArd.

Julie A friend, confidence Keeper, supporter

Amy - Affirming encourager - chAllenge.

Week 2, Day 3

Reading Assignment for the Week: Chapters 3-5

Insights into my private world and my fellowship with Christ:

I struggle To stay called + not driven which
was my parental example.
  Listening To God gives me peace +
perspective - disolues fear of uncertaintx

Insights into serving the cell members and unbelievers in my public world:

I must Take Time To get + keep my
inner world in harmony before I can
Truly serve others.
  I must organize my Time To productively
use iT And provide Time To serve
others.
     I must serve Bill 1ST not LAST.

**Insights into specific cell members or those in their *oikoses* ;
Actions I might take today to serve them:**

Debbie + RhondA, Tony + Mary Beth Tend
To be driven.
  Bill is listening more + will be called
more ofTen.

Week 2, Day 4

Reading Assignment for the Week: Chapters 3-5

Insights into my private world and my fellowship with Christ:

I create such A long list of "To Do"
That sometimes I have Trouble
concentrating when spending quiet/prayer
Time with God.

Insights into serving the cell members and unbelievers in my public world:

Budgeting my Time better will help
me Accomplish key/important interaction
And I will feel more Affirmed.

Insights into specific cell members or those in their *oikoses* ; Actions I might take today to serve them:

Few people know how To budget Their
Time productively. Bill is Among
The best - T.V. is his one weakness.

Week 2, Day 5

Reading Assignment for the Week: Chapters 3-5

Insights into my private world and my fellowship with Christ:

Insights into serving the cell members and unbelievers in my public world:

Insights into specific cell members or those in their *oikoses* ; Actions I might take today to serve them:

Week 3, Day 1

Reading Assignment for the Week: Chapters 6-7

Insights into my private world and my fellowship with Christ:

I need to prioritize my time + actions differently - personal, with God, my job, church. Even job - schedule my duties 1st, help others 2nd.

Insights into serving the cell members and unbelievers in my public world:

Study + prayer will prepare to share better + more effectively.

Insights into specific cell members or those in their *oikoses* ; Actions I might take today to serve them:

Must reach out first to most- especially Julie + Mary Beth.

Week 3, Day 2

Reading Assignment for the Week: Chapters 6-7

Insights into my private world and my fellowship with Christ:

Insights into serving the cell members and unbelievers in my public world:

Insights into specific cell members or those in their *oikoses* ; Actions I might take today to serve them:

Week 3, Day 3

Reading Assignment for the Week: Chapters 6-7

Insights into my private world and my fellowship with Christ:

Insights into serving the cell members and unbelievers in my public world:

Insights into specific cell members or those in their *oikoses* ; Actions I might take today to serve them:

Week 3, Day 4

Reading Assignment for the Week: Chapters 6-7

Insights into my private world and my fellowship with Christ:

Insights into serving the cell members and unbelievers in my public world:

Insights into specific cell members or those in their *oikoses* ; Actions I might take today to serve them:

Week 3, Day 5

Reading Assignment for the Week: Chapters 6-7

Insights into my private world and my fellowship with Christ:

Insights into serving the cell members and unbelievers in my public world:

Insights into specific cell members or those in their *oikoses* ; Actions I might take today to serve them:

Week 4, Day 1

Reading Assignment for the Week: Chapters 8-9

Insights into my private world and my fellowship with Christ:

I need To reAd & discuss insighTs
with others To TrAin my mind.
Also discuss prAyer ThoughTs &
Answers

Insights into serving the cell members and unbelievers in my public world:

I need To chAllenge others To Thiink-
Ask open ended quesTions.

Insights into specific cell members or those in their *oikoses*; Actions I might take today to serve them:

Jimmy is reflecTive of mAny - Debbie
+ RB who do noT reAlly Think buT
mirror conTemporAry culTure.

Week 4, Day 2

Reading Assignment for the Week: Chapters 8-9

Insights into my private world and my fellowship with Christ:

Insights into serving the cell members and unbelievers in my public world:

Insights into specific cell members or those in their *oikoses* ; Actions I might take today to serve them:

Week 4, Day 3

Reading Assignment for the Week: Chapters 8-9

Insights into my private world and my fellowship with Christ:

Insights into serving the cell members and unbelievers in my public world:

Insights into specific cell members or those in their *oikoses* ; Actions I might take today to serve them:

Week 4, Day 4

Reading Assignment for the Week: Chapters 8-9

Insights into my private world and my fellowship with Christ:

Insights into serving the cell members and unbelievers in my public world:

Insights into specific cell members or those in their *oikoses* ; Actions I might take today to serve them:

Week 4, Day 5

Reading Assignment for the Week: Chapters 8-9

Insights into my private world and my fellowship with Christ:

Insights into serving the cell members and unbelievers in my public world:

Insights into specific cell members or those in their *oikoses* ; Actions I might take today to serve them:

Week 5, Day 1

Reading Assignment for the Week: Chapters 10-11

Insights into my private world and my fellowship with Christ:

I felt so wounded The PAST year with my posi-
Tion AT RA I became self centered in A
Survival mode. self protection - I Need To
heal in order To focus on others more Than
myself. I will be A better servant of God.
Mary Beth may be experiencing This now.

Insights into serving the cell members and unbelievers in my public world:

Insights into specific cell members or those in their *oikoses* ; Actions I might take today to serve them:

Week 5, Day 2

Reading Assignment for the Week: Chapters 10-11

Insights into my private world and my fellowship with Christ:

I used To find more Time To spend in prayer & study. I need To limit my energy spent on my job so As To have energy To spend on eTernAl MATTers. I must have responded with more pATience And wisdom.

Insights into serving the cell members and unbelievers in my public world:

Quickly discerning And expressing A Godly perspective KepT my moTives, AcTions And words more Christ-like.

Insights into specific cell members or those in their *oikoses* ; Actions I might take today to serve them:

Debra needs To be encorrAged more To develop her personAl study of God. And noT depend on pASTor's. Bill is growing in wisdom & leAdership As he studies more.

210

Week 5, Day 3

Reading Assignment for the Week: Chapters 10-11

Insights into my private world and my fellowship with Christ:

Insights into serving the cell members and unbelievers in my public world:

Insights into specific cell members or those in their *oikoses* ;
Actions I might take today to serve them:

Week 5, Day 4

Reading Assignment for the Week: Chapters 10-11

Insights into my private world and my fellowship with Christ:

Insights into serving the cell members and unbelievers in my public world:

Insights into specific cell members or those in their *oikoses* ; Actions I might take today to serve them:

Week 5, Day 5

Reading Assignment for the Week: Chapters 10-11

Insights into my private world and my fellowship with Christ:

Insights into serving the cell members and unbelievers in my public world:

Insights into specific cell members or those in their *oikoses* ; Actions I might take today to serve them:

Week 6, Day 1

Reading Assignment for the Week: Chapters 12-13

Insights into my private world and my fellowship with Christ:

My private garden was enough in order
to help me make it through the past
20 months. It is getting overgrown &
needs more cultivation to return
it to the peaceful place it was 2 yrs
ago.

Insights into serving the cell members and unbelievers in my public world:

Very few have a healthy private
garden. Those that appear to are:
Janet, Robbie, Andrea, Robin, Kathy — I
need to spend more time with them.
Many more people appear to have their
public world in order.

Insights into specific cell members or those in their oikoses ; Actions I might take today to serve them:

Julie draws upon Janet's garden as
Bill used to draw on mine. Randy draws
on Jimmy's. We should discuss the
importance of our own garden being
cultivated & not drawing on some one elses.
Toni is working in hers & needs encouragem
I don't understand Amy's but she seems God
lead.

214

Week 6, Day 2

Reading Assignment for the Week: Chapters 12-13

Insights into my private world and my fellowship with Christ:

Insights into serving the cell members and unbelievers in my public world:

Insights into specific cell members or those in their *oikoses* ; Actions I might take today to serve them:

Week 6, Day 3

Reading Assignment for the Week: Chapters 12-13

Insights into my private world and my fellowship with Christ:

Insights into serving the cell members and unbelievers in my public world:

Insights into specific cell members or those in their *oikoses* ; Actions I might take today to serve them:

Week 6, Day 4

Reading Assignment for the Week: Chapters 12-13

Insights into my private world and my fellowship with Christ:

Insights into serving the cell members and unbelievers in my public world:

Insights into specific cell members or those in their *oikoses* ; Actions I might take today to serve them:

Week 6, Day 5

Reading Assignment for the Week: Chapters 12-13

Insights into my private world and my fellowship with Christ:

Insights into serving the cell members and unbelievers in my public world:

Insights into specific cell members or those in their *oikoses* ; Actions I might take today to serve them:

Week 7, Day 1

Reading Assignment for the Week: Chapter 14

Insights into my private world and my fellowship with Christ:

Insights into serving the cell members and unbelievers in my public world:

Insights into specific cell members or those in their *oikoses* ; Actions I might take today to serve them:

Week 7, Day 2

Reading Assignment for the Week: Chapter 14

Insights into my private world and my fellowship with Christ:

Insights into serving the cell members and unbelievers in my public world:

Insights into specific cell members or those in their *oikoses* ; Actions I might take today to serve them:

Week 7, Day 3

Reading Assignment for the Week: Chapter 14

Insights into my private world and my fellowship with Christ:

Insights into serving the cell members and unbelievers in my public world:

Insights into specific cell members or those in their *oikoses* ; Actions I might take today to serve them:

Week 7, Day 4

Reading Assignment for the Week: Chapter 14

Insights into my private world and my fellowship with Christ:

Insights into serving the cell members and unbelievers in my public world:

Insights into specific cell members or those in their *oikoses* ; Actions I might take today to serve them:

Week 7, Day 5

Reading Assignment for the Week: Chapter 14

Insights into my private world and my fellowship with Christ:

Insights into serving the cell members and unbelievers in my public world:

**Insights into specific cell members or those in their *oikoses* ;
Actions I might take today to serve them:**

Week 8, Day 1

Reading Assignment for the Week: End Pages

Insights into my private world and my fellowship with Christ:

Insights into serving the cell members and unbelievers in my public world:

Insights into specific cell members or those in their *oikoses* ; Actions I might take today to serve them:

Week 8, Day 2

Reading Assignment for the Week: End Pages

Insights into my private world and my fellowship with Christ:

Insights into serving the cell members and unbelievers in my public world:

Insights into specific cell members or those in their *oikoses* ; Actions I might take today to serve them:

Week 8, Day 3

Reading Assignment for the Week: End Pages

Insights into my private world and my fellowship with Christ:

Insights into serving the cell members and unbelievers in my public world:

Insights into specific cell members or those in their *oikoses* ; Actions I might take today to serve them:

Week 8, Day 4

Reading Assignment for the Week: End Pages

Insights into my private world and my fellowship with Christ:

Insights into serving the cell members and unbelievers in my public world:

Insights into specific cell members or those in their *oikoses* ; Actions I might take today to serve them:

Week 8, Day 5

Reading Assignment for the Week: End Pages

Insights into my private world and my fellowship with Christ:

Insights into serving the cell members and unbelievers in my public world:

Insights into specific cell members or those in their *oikoses* ; Actions I might take today to serve them: